D1712772

# Walking
# in
# Missionary
# Shoes

# Walking in Missionary Shoes:

## A History of the Church of God in Kenya, East Africa (1905-1970)

by Lima Lehmer Williams

Published by
Warner Press, Inc.
Anderson, Indiana

*Dedicated to those men and women, both living and dead, who walked the paths of Kenya, serving more than a thousand years to make this story possible.*

# Contents

# Foreword

Lima Lehmer Williams, author of this fascinating storybook history of the Church of God in Kenya from 1905 to 1970, was caught up in its development in 1936. Highly dedicated and motivated for missionary service, she poured out her life during the thirty years she labored in Kenya—enough time to give authenticity to her observations and comments.

Lima relates this saga through stories told by missionaries, African Christians, and herself. It relates her own pilgrimage through missionary experiences. There are places in this book wherein she used vocabulary of that period that today might be considered degrading or colonial. These statements are not meant to be offensive or derogatory.

The reader needs to remember that the people of Kenya developed during those years from a very primitive way of life. Gradually but surely changes took place affecting their entire culture. This steady progress was initiated and sustained by missionaries, assisted by a colonial government, and subsequently propelled toward self-reliance by the Africans themselves, especially following their conversion to Christianity and their independence from colonial rule. The people of Kenya have now become able persons in a modern society while maintaining many wonderful characteristics of their own heritage and culture.

The Church of God in Kenya has continued rapid progress during the past fifteen years since Lima left. It has more trained and capable African leaders. Church of God missionaries are today in Kenya to assist in some specialized services only by request of the African church. The Church of God in East Africa is engaged in missionary outreach into other African countries south of the Sahara. Sometimes this is in partnership with the church in America.

The African church will continue to develop, move, forward, and grow, but only as Africans will do it and not as American missionaries would have done it through a controlled mission.

And who is to say the African way is wrong when different? There will be some failures and shortcomings in this forward movement, just as there were when the mission was in control.

I have been privileged to follow Lima throughout her career, having been appointed three years earlier than she to missionary service and through having been secretary-treasurer of the Missionary Board from 1954 to 1975. What she has written is authentic. Many times it is written through the eyes of missionaries newly arrived to Kenya, as in her own case. You will observe the tremendous influence Lima had during her years of consecrated helpfulness among the Africans. And they loved her!

Happy reading. Enjoy the stories. You may gain some insights into missionary life you never imagined existed. Perhaps a young reader might become interested in missionary service, even though the situations facing a missionary today are quite different from the days of Lima's experiences.

—Lester A. Crose
Retired missiologist

# Preface

After reading of the tremendous outreach program of the Church of God in East Africa as it broke through tribal boundaries into Kisii, Masai, Uganda, and Tanzania, I was inspired to write this record of those who led the way for the self-sustaining church. Many of the chief players in this activity have long ago passed on to their heavenly reward. Yet their history has been unrecorded.

Through letters, tapes, telephone calls, and personal contacts, the materials so graciously shared have formed the content of this book. Much of the material has been obtained from contemporaries of those who have gone on, but whose memories should live with the church; not as marbled saints, for none of them could be called saintly. They were human beings who were challenged by success and failure, joy and sorrow, sickness, health, even death, discouragement, inconvenience, and separation from their children and families. They were dedicated to carry the gospel over and beyond the ordinary borders of Christian witness.

Although an attempt has been made to follow the development of the Mission in Kenya Colony, later known as Kenya, I am describing this development primarily through the human experiences of the missionaries and their families who have spent more than a total of one thousand years of missionary service from the beginning to the end of this story.

The mission development has not always been spectacular, but it has shown steady growth. Through God's help, it superseded, to quote the Apostle Paul, "all that we could have asked or thought." The Luyia-speaking people have been very responsive to the gospel message. The eagerness and faithfulness of the first-generation Christians planted a steadfastness in the church that has never been surpassed by any group of people. From the beginning, they became a true, faithful, and hard-working congregation of Christians.

Now as we reach the stage at which the mission no longer exists and the birth of a self-reliant church extends itself into other tribal and language areas, our prayers and encouragement go with them.

A word of appreciation should be given to the younger generation of African leaders. They have sacrificed many years overseas to attain adequate training to lead the new church into realms that never could have been reached by foreigners. The enthusiasm and splendid preparation, combined with divine dedication, should challenge both leaders and congregations to extend the church far and wide throughout Africa.

One factor that has been so favorable in the Luyia-speaking church has been the unity that has never encouraged division or breaking away. They have always maintained a spirit of united effort that has held the church together.

May it always be so.

# Acknowledgements

The author would like to express thanks and appreciation for the information received by tapes, letters, telephone calls, and interviews from the following: Irene Engst, Margaret and Frank LaFont; Nora and Ruben Schwieger; Glenna Yutzy; Vera Martin; Hazel (McDilda) Cage; Lydia (Hansen) McDonald; Calvin and Martha Brallier; Sidney Rogers; Charles Ludwig; Revere Cook; and Alberta Baker. I am also indebted to her sister, the late Mabel Baker, who through the years inspired me to write this history. Then I shall be eternally grateful to Mrs. Myrna Mitchell, the daughter of Edgar and Mildred Williams, who typed the manuscript.

Thanks to Bensen Ndebe for the fine information he shared of the progress of the African Church of God, and to Byrum Makokha for the splendid reports that he gave through the various publications.

A very deep sense of appreciation goes to Obed Kutera and the Kisii elders, who opened Kisii to the church and helped us through so many of the very difficult choices necessary.

And last of all, for my husband's patience with my curtailing many of the other activities in which we ordinarily participated.

May God bless all of you as we join together in continued prayer for the African church.

# Introduction

The smoky fire was reduced to a few smoldering ashes. Chuma picked up a handful of dried cow dung and placed it on the few dying sparks.

Crossing her arms across her naked chest, she shivered as she returned to the side of her very ill husband who lay groaning on the cow's-hide pallet on the bare floor. Otinga's breathing was quick and raspy. He coughed continuously. As Chuma placed her hand on his chest, she realized that his heartbeat was becoming weaker.

Nudging her eldest son, now asleep by her side, she nodded pointing her chin toward his father.

"He's getting weaker; the end is near," she said.

Anyamba moved next to his father as he rubbed his sleepy eyes.

"Yes," he replied.

Thoughts began to torment Chuma as she relived the days of the past moon.

Did we do all there was to do for him? she asked herself. The witch doctor came and killed the white goat I begged from my father. He did the sacrifice to the two dead ancestors, whom he said were troubling us because we had forgotten them."

She reached down and touched the still-wet strip of the skin of the slaughtered goat that was tied around his wrists as a fetish to ward off more trouble.

The father's breathing became heavier and the rattle in his throat became more alarming.

"Mama, did you call the medicine man?"

"Oh, yes. Don't you see the puncture wound he made between his ribs to release the fluid from his chest?"

"What about the magic finder? Perhaps one of father's enemies planted some article near the garden to bewitch him."

"Yes, Simekha came yesterday and he dug up his old teeth

which he found buried in the path. He removed it to break the spell that the person with the lame foot put on him."

"Everything has been done that we know how to do. We must just wait."

"Did your father give you the sacrifice stone from his altar before he became ill? He wanted to do so for a long time," said Chuma.

"Yes, he did, but I have been waiting to transplant it with the other two stones in my yard until the *obuli* [grain] is harvested. We will need to make a feast and have plenty of beer."

All at once as they spoke, Otinga sat up, gasped, and fell back on the pallet, dead.

Chuma let out a shriek and began to wail as she picked her husband up by the shoulders, and dropped him quickly.

"*Ndakhakhola mbwena*" [What will I do]? Who will eat my *obusuma* [food]? Who will cut the grass in the garden? Who will repair my roof?" she sang between wails.

Up and down the path she ran, screaming and wailing to the top of her voice. By now all of the nearby neighbors were awakened and they continued the mourning cry as they rushed up and down the narrow paths leading to Otinga's house. The hut was soon crowded with people crying, screaming, as they placed their hands back and forth over their mouths, emitting a weird penetrating cry that was heard for miles.

The drummer soon appeared to announce the death. The rest of the night was spent in wailing and beating the drum. Its constant repetition awakened even the sleepiest one as the sound reverberated over the hillsides and down to the most remote valley.

This was a big day, a historic day, for Otinga was a great man. His five sons moved about the hut getting ready for the funeral. Otinga's four daughters must be notified. All of them lived in villages quite a distance from home, so a runner was sent to carry the message.

The yard and house were crowded with people—children, grandchildren, nieces and nephews, young, old, and middle-aged. No one would dare to remain from the funeral lest he or she be called a witch or the person who put a spell on the deceased one. It was not only a sad event but a great social one.

The men of the clan had another obligation—to organize the *esilemba* [funeral dance]. Dusting off their spears and shields, feathered head pieces, and monkey skins, they proceeded to find as much of the colored mud as they could and daubed themselves. Their hideous appearance was thought to drive away the evil spirits so that they would not return to take another life. Their blackened eyes, yellow arms, white and brown mud-streaked nude bodies shook as they began to dance.

The more important the deceased, the more who came to help drive away the evil spirits. Otinga's cows were brought from the various grazing places, decked out with bells and long strands of a creeping vine draped around their necks. The cows preceded the *esilemba* as they were chased hurriedly down the paths.

What a motley group of former warriors who had fought with Otinga. Their ballads were sung about his bravery as they raced down every important path through the many villages shaking their spears as if charging the evil spirits. Frightened little children ran behind the bushes to peer out through the branches. This was the day of days, one long to be remembered!

Every new baby born during this period of mourning was named for the great warrior who lay in state before his house. Because their history was as yet unrecorded, the date of a death was remembered by the birth of the child.

By the following day the time of burial was long overdue according to our customs, but because many of the relatives lived a distance away, the interment was delayed of necessity until all arrived.

All day and all night long, they danced, sang, and ate whatever could be found. The grain bins would be empty by the time all the guests had gone home. Little thought was given to the needs of the remaining widow.

Children played, old friends had time to visit, young people met and spun yarns, and perhaps business deals or marriage arrangements were made at this time of freedom. Oftentimes quarrels began if accusations were made.

As the cows preceded the *esilemba* driven by the sons and followed behind with the warriors running at top speed, the people stepped aside to let them pass like a famous parade. The widow sat on her stool facing the group. She slowly rose to meet them.

She had been a good faithful wife and with a clear conscience she could face them and the evil spirits. Had she been unfaithful to her husband, she would have turned her back to them and faced the wall—so great was their belief in the evil spirits.

After a grand parade of show, the members of the *esilemba* rushed back and forth in the yard pretending to pierce the evil spirits with their spears. Everyone gave them adequate room as they watched the procession. Various ones stood over the bier and wailed and screamed, keeping the entire place in a disorganized frenzy. The time came to bury the great one. The shallow grave, which had been dug during the night, was lined with banana leaves. Then Otinga's body was laid in a fetal position in the grave. They were sure to place a leaf in his ear so that he could still hear what was going on in the world he was leaving. The deceased ancestors were felt to be still a part of the society and were just as important as the living beings.

When the grave was finally covered, someone climbed to the roof of the house, removed the center stick of the hut, and placed it on the grave with some of his other choice possessions that he used frequently.

The group began their journey home and the *esilemba* ran back to their villages. Each morning the family and especially the wife continued to run down the path and wail as she sang a ballad about her husband. The remainder of the time she sat at her hut and received condolences.

Her eldest son was now responsible for her and would be her guardian, managing the family's affairs. Had she no adult sons, then her husband's brother would take responsibility for her and her family. In most instances he would take her for his wife.

# Part One:
## The Early Years in Kenya Colony

### Chapter 1

# How It All Began

The year 1983 was a great one for the African Church of God in Kenya and Tanzania. In that year the World Conference of the Church of God was held for the first time in Nairobi, Kenya. The African churches were able to give a tangible indication to the conference of what God had done for them since their beginnings seventy-eight years earlier.

But I am afraid most of you missed some of the more exciting landmarks if you came by air. Just think how much more interesting travel over land on foot would have been with a string of porters carrying all the earthly possessions you hoped to need for the next seven years. After all, the trip is six-hundred miles from Mombasa, the seaport.

We would hope that you would have been able to see all the unmarked graves of many of the porters and missionaries who did not complete the journey.

A few early attempts were made at missions as far up from the coast as the Kikuyu land, but a lasting work did not reach the eastern side of Lake Victoria until after the railroad was extended to Kisumu.

In 1897 a young man named Peter Scott left a West African mission to come to Kijabe, hoping to establish a link of missions across Africa. He became the founder of the African

1

Inland Mission. Although Mr. Scott tried very hard to accomplish his objective, he died a year later. During his year there he was said to have traveled twenty-six hundred miles on foot to plant the gospel message, walking forty-five miles on the day before he died.

Another group of twelve missionaries followed him, though in a few years only one, Mr. Hotchkiss, remained.

The director, C. G. Hulbert, was joined by Mr. Johnstone. These men attempted to use the Kikuyu language, which was better accepted than Swahili at that time. The African Inland Mission began to experience some success. Mr. Hulburt later brought his family and engaged in a very effective work.

A few books of the New Testament had been translated and printed as well as a pamphlet entitled *Hearing and Doing,* which reached Robert Wilson, a missionary working in South Africa under the South African Mines Compound.

When the Robert Wilsons heard of the great need in British East Africa, they felt called of God to go to minister to the people there. He told A. W. Baker, the director and founder of the compound, about his calling. Although the need for workers in South Africa was great, Mr. Baker was very sympathetic and understanding, and he asked them to pray about it.

A. W. Baker of South Africa, founder of the Kima Mission, was an attorney. He worked to evangelize the Zulus. These South African tribesmen were brought to Johannesburg and the surrounding areas to work in the mines where they often fell into degradation and misery. He writes,

> *Over one hundred thousand of the finest young men of our natives [were] gathered in compounds along a stretch of about sixty miles on the outcrop of the Gold Reefs, where they were being demoralized by drink, gambling, and other European vices.*
>
> *Being in Johannesburg on a certain Sunday in 1895, I went down in the City and Suburban Gold Mine, gathered a group of some two hundred . . . together in the open air, and preached the gospel to them. At the close, half a dozen came into the ring as penitants. One of these, with streaming eyes said, "Umfundishi [teacher], here we are far from our homes and surrounded by all sorts of temptations. No man cares for our souls. You can speak our language. Will you not come and be our shepherd?"*
>
> *My thoughts traveled along the reef, and I began to appreciate the fact that it was the finest seedbed in South Africa.*

## Chapter 2

# Robert Wilson
# Explores the Land

When the conference of the South African Compound and Interior Mission met, Robert Wilson summed up his argument about going north to British East Africa in A. W. Baker's book *Grace Abounding:*

*The Johannesburg Compounds furnish a splendid field of work. They are not fully evangelized, but the natives here have the opportunity of hearing the word of God; there they do not. Someone should go. I am young and strong and more suitable than new arrivals unclimatized. My knowledge of Zulu and Sesuto will help me pick up the language.*

The conference was unanimous in encouraging the Bakers. Mr. Baker reiterated Mr. Wilson's language qualifications indicating him to be especially fitted to acquire the Kavirondo dialect, which seems to be a combination of the two languages, or a closely related one since it was a Bantu language. Mrs. Wilson was rugged and had been a colonist. The children were not spoiled. The Wilsons were seen as the best family to go. So Robert was sent forth on a trip of exploration.

When Mr. Wilson arrived at Mombasa, he took the train to

Kijabe, the source of the pamphlet *Hearing and Doing*, which had influenced Mrs. Wilson and him to come. Here he met C. S. Hulburt, the head of the African Inland Mission. Mr. Hulburt was very enthusiastic about the prospects for mission work in East Africa. He shared his plans of having a connecting link of missions extending along the Nile River. Mr. Wilson was very much impressed but he continued on his journey to Port Florence (Kisumu). There he found only a small place with a few Banyan stores, a couple of forwarding agents, government buildings, commissioner's house, and a post office.

From Kisumu he began his walk of twenty miles to the Friends African Mission at Kaimosi. The mission was only about three years old but about fifty Africans were at work making bricks, constructing roads, and generally getting things in order. The missionaries were living in grass houses until the brick ones could be erected.

Although Mr. Wilson had been a seasoned missionary in South Africa, he experienced a series of culture shocks. He had not encountered the local customs elsewhere. Nor had he come in contact with the soldier ants that seemed to be everywhere. The first night he was there, two of the missionaries' houses had to be vacated when the ants forced them out.

"Don't these people ever wear clothes?" he asked Mr. Reese, a Friends missionary.

"These people have never seen clothes before we came," Mr. Reese replied. "They have always lived here and have learned to live with the things they were able to provide for themselves. Many of them die of exposure, for the nights here are very cold, and without blankets they become chilled. If the malaria doesn't take them, other respiratory illnesses will."

"Well," said Mr. Wilson, "one of the first things I want to do is to put clothes on them. I wouldn't want my boys to see them."

"None of us like it," Mr. Reese replied, "but we are becoming accustomed to it and as soon as it is practical we will try to put clothing on them. We must be careful not to introduce American or European customs instead of Christianity to them."

"What about the language? Do you have any means of communicating with them? They don't seem to respond to Swahili."

"Very true. Swahili is the coastal language and only those who have gone up-country would know it. I have been trying to compile a vocabulary, but as yet it is quite limited."

"I trust you will be able to share it with me when we come," Mr. Wilson implored.

4

"I surely will; there are so few of us here now that we must share and share alike. Here is a small suggestion about learning the language. These people never point with their finger. They point with their chin. I was trying to find out a certain word and kept pointing with my finger. Each time they gave me the word for finger. I said, 'What is this?' Each time they replied *'esitera'* or finger. Then one time I saw them bending down and laughing at me. That was a good joke. To think the white man had no more sense than that. It took a long time before the meaning came through, but when it did, I laughed at myself with them. It broke the ice when we could laugh together. They are good people, Mr. Wilson, and we have already learned to love them."

The next day the commissioner came by and told us that the Nandi were having a short war. He suggested that all the women and children move to Marigoli. So it gave Mr. Wilson the opportunity he was looking for. Mr. Willis from the Church Missionary Society had a mission in Marigoli territory. So he took Mr. Wilson out to explore the land. Prior to that time some had wanted to go to the Kabras area. But the government official did not think it would be healthy enough for women and children.

Mr. Willis and Mr. Wilson began their long walk toward the west. They came upon an elevated territory in Bunyore. As they looked around, they found that it was not only a healthy area, but that it was very densely populated. The major obstacle was a water supply but several springs were located at the bottom of the hill.

"Let's go to see the chief, Otieno," Mr. Willis said.

They came to the village where the chief lived. Several little children were playing in the yard. As soon as they saw the white men approaching, the children ran and hid. The very young began to scream and cry, for the older girls who cared for them had often told them the white man would eat them if they were bad.

After hearing the commotion and noise of the children crying and chickens scattering and squawking, the old chief came out slowly, putting on his chieftain's cap as he walked.

*"Milembe,"* said Mr. Willis.

*"Milembe,"* he answered as he shook hands with the two men.

They explained as well as they could, partly in Swahili and partly in Luragoli, the purpose of their mission. Otieno was very cordial and told them how happy he would be to have a

5

mission in his area. He was a progressive man who had little use for the God they represented, but he had heard of the progress they brought to the people. Yes, he would agree for a mission to begin in his territory and would certainly help all he could. The missionaries were very pleased with these arrangements.

After making arrangements with the proper government authorities, he began his journey back to South Africa, spending Christmas with his newfound friends, Mr. and Mrs. Hulbert, in Kijabe. He knew now that Kima was the place for Mrs. Wilson and himself.

Mr. Baker urged them to prepare and go forth.

# Chapter 3

# The Wilsons Arrive at Kima

The Robert Wilsons and their two sons, Harland and Robert, finally arrived on the new railway at Kisumu (Port Florence) with a limited amount of household equipment. Try to imagine this brave little family as they faced a journey of some twenty miles to the Friends Mission at Kaimosi. From Kisumu on, they could only travel by foot. Mrs. Wilson, who was pregnant at the time, was transported in a carrying chair, commonly used in that day for the transportation of women missionaries. Its two poles were carried either in the hands or on the shoulders of four porters. Another such as this may have been provided for the little boys. Mr. Wilson proceeded on foot. Uganda porters carried up to a sixty-pound load of possessions on their heads.

They finally arrived in Kaimosi where they pitched their tent until they could get to Kima. Because of a tribal uprising, they soon went to Marigoli and then shortly on to Kima.

On August 15, 1905, the Wilsons left Marigoli, taking their two sons and the Baganda porters, a tent, and sufficient food for a few days.

Their first task was to build shelters of poles and grass to house the porters and their provisions.

Mrs. Wilson bought bunches of thatching grass from the people, using salt as a medium for trade. Chief Otieno helped them find poles and persuaded the men to bring them to Mr. Wilson in exchange for *pice*, the local currency.

At first the women and girls were very shy and the slightest move would send them scurrying away.

On August 20, the missionaries' first Sunday, they would not buy the grass that the people came to sell. On God's special day they raised a white flag, put on their best clothes, and Mrs. Wilson brought out her harmonium and began to play. The dozen bystanders increased rapidly to a large group of about one hundred.

How handicapped they felt. Plenty of people stood by, but they did not have the language for preaching to them. While they knew the Bantu language of a certain area, yet more than a thousand Bantu languages were spoken. Most of them have common underlying construction, but each differs from the others.

With Mr. Reese's Friends missionary vocabulary of Marigoli and their Zulu background, they were soon able to translate a few simple songs. Nothing could have pleased the Africans more. They loved to sing. Soon the songs could be heard everywhere.

In due time a twelve-by-twelve-foot mud and pole house had been completed for the Wilsons; it served as a store, pantry, dining room, and all else. A larger one was under construction. When the rains began in September, they had no choice except to close the windows and remain in the dark, or to keep shifting from one open window to another as the wind changed.

"I thought we were living on the equator," Mr. Wilson said to his wife.

"You wouldn't think so to feel this chilly weather," she replied as she pulled her shawl closer to her.

The rain was blowing in through the wooden shutters on the east side, water was trickling down the wall, and the red mud became softer and softer until finally a little stream ran over the cowdung-plastered floor.

"What can we use to fill those cracks in the shutters?" she asked. "If I could find a tree with some pitch in it, that would do the trick. Oh, to be able to speak and ask these fellows."

"Tomorrow I'll try to find something," Mr. Wilson said. "This rain will make our floor as muddy as the puddle the boys just ran through outside. We do need a permanent house. With the baby on the way, I would like you to have a better place than this."

"I suppose Mary would have been happy to have had this much when Jesus was born," she said as she smiled kindly at him. "We haven't been sick. We have so much to be thankful for. Otieno has cooperated with us by sending poles to buy. With so few trees in the community, one wonders where they all come from."

"That certainly presents another problem," he said. "Without trees or wood, we will not be able to burn bricks. I must write Mr. Baker about a house. The Friends Mission is built in the midst of a huge forest where there are plenty of trees and enough wood to last for years to come, but their people are scattered. It is the people we came for."

At last the rain stopped. They opened the windows and everything looked so fresh outside. The sun was shining again. Just over the hill was a complete rainbow. The boys were excited, for never before had they seen the full circle of the rainbow, so typical on the equator.

"Is there a pot of gold at both ends?" Robert asked.

"Someday we'll go to see," said his brother, Harland. "Let's mark the rocks where it ends and we'll try to find the pot of gold."

"What would you buy if you could find it?"

"A trip back to see grandma and grandpa, and all the lads we left behind," he said with a big sigh.

## Chapter 4

# Johanna Bila

When the Wilsons were ready to leave for their new field of labor, Johanna Bila, a young convert from one of the South African Compound and Interior Missions, also felt the call of God to go to this unevangelized tribe in British East Africa. Knowing of Bila's enthusiasm, Mr. Baker sent him to work with the Wilson family. He was an unmarried Zulu who gave himself unstintingly to the work. His background in another Bantu language facilitated his acquiring the language quickly, and first Christians will never forget the impact he made on them.

He soon began teaching reading. When the hour arrived for the people to return from their gardens, Johanna could be seen starting off to visit them in their yards. He missed no opportunity of preaching to them and repeating that old familiar story still so new to the Bunyore people.

Yet he was not always cordially received. The following testimony was given by one of the candidates for baptism many years later.

*On one occasion I was very sick, and the witch doctor was dosing me with medicine and rubbing powders into incisions in my skin when Johanna appeared at the door. I swore at him and ordered him to be off. He, however, sat down and said,*

*"There is only one who can cure sickness because he is the giver of life. His name is Jesus. That witch doctor is a servant of Satan, the one who brought death into the world. His medicine will do you no good."*

*I refused to listen but drove him away. The medicines did me no good and I grew steadily worse. I was lying at the point of death. One day Johanna walked in again. Sitting down he said to me, "I told you that Satan could not cure you. He will surely kill you; but Jesus is the Son of God and is able and willing to cure the body and save the soul. If you will let me collect and burn all these medicines and garments of prayer to the spirits of your departed ancestors, I will pray to him and he will heal you."*

*I thought I was dying anyway. The medicines had done me no good, and his praying could do me no harm, so I consented. Johanna collected all the heathen charms and medicines and made a bonfire of them. Then he knelt and prayed for me and I recovered and began to follow Jesus. I continued for a short time and then old temptations returned and I went back to my old sins; but the day that they buried Johanna's body, I came back to the Lord Jesus and have never gone back since.*

One day while Johanna Bila was thatching a roof he fell off. From then on his strength began to diminish and he became very frail due to miner's tuberculosis. In spite of his weakness he never forgot his call, and his zeal never ceased toward reaching those to whom he had been sent. His sermons were frequently interrupted by spasms of coughing; however, he preached on until he could no longer leave his bed.

A few of the earlier Christians mourned his death and have never forgotten his usefulness. Many of those who witnessed the burial of their first Christian missionaries have since embraced that gospel that was so real to Johanna. A story related by one of the early Christians portrayed Johanna's patience and love for planting the gospel:

*He had planted a garden of peanuts, but as fast as they grew the neighbors dug them up and stole them. He never said a word but replanted them and continued to do so until the day of his death.*

The name of Johanna Bila was spoken softly and with the deepest reverence by all the early Christians.

# Chapter 5

# A Trip to Kisumu

"*T*he draft came yesterday for the lumber and the building materials," Robert Wilson said to his wife. "I want to leave before the sun comes up and take the porters with me to carry the materials back home. Don't expect us back until the following day. It will take the rest of tomorrow to run around and find the kind of beams we need. We'll put up somewhere for the night, so don't worry about us."

"Be sure to measure the meal tonight for the porters," Mrs. Wilson replied, "or you will get a late start. It seems as if the rains begin earlier every day. I'll have your tea and breakfast about five. You had better take a lunch and a bottle of cold tea. Where will the porters get their food?"

"They will carry it with them and cook wherever they can find a place," he answered. "There seems to be plenty of sticks near the town that they can use for fuel. I'll buy something in the store and may find a good friend who will put me up for the night. You won't be afraid, will you?"

"No, of course not," she said.

Early the next morning, with fifty Buganda porters following him, he rode his bicycle down the path toward Kisumu.

The descent was not too bad, but as they reached the scorching plains, they looked for water. The only water available was in a muddy pool where a herd of cattle were standing, swishing away the flies with their tails. Mr. Wilson took a sip of the cold tea from the bottle his wife had prepared for him. The porters all ran toward the pool, chasing the cows in every direction. They doused themselves from head to foot with the water, trying to cool off their hot bodies. Then they found a small trickle of cleaner water at the side of the pool where they could get a drink. Refreshed, they now continued across the hot plain leading into Kisumu.

After about three and a half hours of walking, the town could be seen at the side of Lake Victoria. A shady place was soon found where they could lie down and rest. Then Mr. Wilson hunted for his building materials.

The next morning the few Asian storekeepers began dealing out the sixty-pound loads for each porter to carry. The long beams and boards were shared between two carriers. Kegs of nails, tools, and cement found other takers. Those who carried the long metal sheets of iron for the roof were among the most fortunate ones later on.

On their long, hot homeward trail across the plain they began a slow ascent from an elevation of 4,000 feet up to 5,200 feet back to Kima.

Two hours from Kisumu, thunder began to roar and the sky darkened. Their steps quickened, but no matter how fast they walked the rain overtook them.

Mr. Wilson's bicycle became a burden by this time. Sometimes he pushed it and other times he carried it through the sticky red mud. The feet of the caravan slipped and slid through flashing lightning and exploding thunder. The only wayside shelters were the scrubby bushes. The men kept moving as the rain ran down their faces, half blinding them. Finally after an hour, the rain began to slow down. The sun came out and everything looked bright again. The group of porters did what they always do when faced with a difficult task; they sang. The leader began and the rest followed in a chorus as they kept moving. Before they realized it, they were dry and very near the mission. Perhaps Mr. Wilson did not dry as quickly since he had more clothing to dry. We hoped the bags of cement did not solidify before they could be used.

Chapter 6

# The People Sing

With the days of their worst frustrations behind, prospects began to look much brighter for the Wilsons. Although they were still living in temporary quarters, they had adjusted very well to the situation. Mr. Wilson declared, "The bread that Mrs. Wilson baked over three stones on the floor of her kitchen, with a covered pot over the top for an oven, was just as good as any from a fine bakery." Even the rain did not appear as a trial any longer.

Mr. Wilson was soon able to discontinue the use of the Baganda porters. The men had moved nearer to the mission and now were able to speak to each other a little, even though still greatly limited because of the language barrier.

How they enjoyed the songs that had been translated into their language. "Jesus Is Calling" rang throughout the hillsides as they sat at their fires during the leisure evening hours. They still were unable to understand the message the missionary was trying to give them about a future life with God. They laughed and said that they would never see their dead ancestors. One man said he would like to be God's cook if there was such a position in heaven.

Then in November Mr. Bertson came from South Africa to help build the mission house. How excited the Wilsons became. But even missionaries have disappointments. After the men met at the station with their usual greetings, Mr. Wilson asked if he had received the list of materials that he sent through a friend. As Mr. Wilson looked at the straw hat Mr. Bertson was wearing, he felt certain that something had gone amiss.

"No, I haven't seen or heard from him for a long time," Mr. Bertson replied.

"Then you did not bring the tools and the rest of the equipment I needed," Mr. Wilson said. "Did you bring a helmet for this hot sun? We are on the equator and must protect ourselves from its intense rays when we work outside. I just do not know where we can buy one in this country. We will certainly have to send immediately to Mombasa to get you one. Let's fill your hat with leaves to insulate it," he said as they began to cross the plains enroute home.

Poor Mr. Bertson soon understood what he meant, for long before he arrived at the mission, the back of his neck was aching. All through the night he was up and down with nausea and extreme headache. Heat stroke was a great hazard of walking twenty miles in the African sun.

When he unpacked his small suitcase, the much-needed trowel was certainly not in evidence. Even if by some unlikely miracle they would have one in Kisumu, it meant a forty-mile trip on foot or bike to get it.

"Come and see our bricks that the workers have made," Mr. Wilson said. We have twenty-thousand drying in the shed ready for the house. The men are carrying stones from the nearby hills for the foundation of the house. It is a long process, but the pile is growing. A man may walk several miles to find a large stone and then he brings one at a time. Not very progressive, but we must have patience."

That night little Thelma Wilson became the newest member of our missionary family. Mrs. Blackburn from the Friends African Mission came to be with the courageous mother.

# Chapter 7

# Children Serve, Too

**M**rs. Wilson persuaded a young girl to take care of the baby. She required the girl to bathe each day and wear clothing. In later years after this nurse child had become a Christian, she laughed as she told us about her first mission experiences. She said, "I could not stand the smell of soap. When I went home each evening I crushed the piece of cloth up and put it in the water pot until the next morning, and then I'd shake it out again and tie it over my shoulder." This young woman became one of the first Christians.

The children of missionaries had a great influence on the African children and often become good friends with them. The American or foreign children learned the language very readily from the native children. One little girl who had been on the mission from the age of three years was often able to explain the meaning of words to her mother.

Here is an imaginary story about an African child who was curious about what were sometimes called "rat tracks."

### Do Rat Tracks Really Talk?

*"Today I'm going down to see the white man do his magic,"* murmured Anyambo to his half brother across the garden as they took their cows to pasture.

*"A white man! Whoever saw a white man? Is he an Albino*

like Omulafu?" shouted Kitu.

"No," said Anyambo. "He came across the water far from here. He's calling the people to that funny little house he built with three sides. Let's go; they say he gives us peanuts."

"If he gives us peanuts we can't miss it," Kitu decided at once. "And now since this isn't the flying ant season, I'll be starving after herding cows all day."

"Well, we won't go close to him," Anyambo cautioned, "for the old folks say he'll eat you. We must be very careful."

"I'll just hold out my hand real far and you stand near me," Kitu said. "If he grabs me, you pull me back quickly. What sort of magic does he do?"

"He makes rat tracks on a board and says they talk," Anyambo explained. "Some boys and even the girl who works for his family go about saying, 'ba, be, bi, bo, bu.' I suppose he is teaching them his language, for he can't talk to us. You must see him. He has long hair and even has hair on his arms. His wife and boys have long straight hair and the mother has very long hair, much longer than the hair on the cow's tail. All of them keep their bodies covered with what the village elders who have been away from home call clothing. Some say their feet look like cow's feet—they have hooves. I wonder if they have toes like ours. They seem to have fingers but do they really have toes?"

"Let's call the other boys to come with us in case he grabs one of us," Kitu suggested. "The others can wail and that will bring the people to our rescue."

So Anyamba and Kitu spread the news to the other herd boys as they went to the valley to herd their cows. They soon forgot the white man and Kitu began making a slide down a slippery hill, using the halves of an old banana tree trunk. After splitting it in two pieces, they each had a sled which they used to slide down the hill. Their brown bodies were soon splattered with mud, but with the river so near there was no problem. Hunger pangs reminded them that game would taste good if they could only hunt some. At first all they found was a nice fat grasshopper; then Kitu did find a small quail. Securing it well to a small bush, he proceeded to gather the sticks necessary for a fire.

Anyamba soon returned with a stick and stones and some very dry leaves which he crumbled as the boys proceeded to use the age-old method of making fire. While Anyamba twirled the stick very fast between the palms of his hands, Kitu put his face down near the ground and blew gently and patiently until *he saw the first spark. Quickly they added more crushed leaves. Soon they had a fire.*

*"Now get the wet clay and wrap it around the quail with a leaf and we'll soon have a delicious morsel," said Anyamba. Kitu returned from the river with the quail dripping with mud, wrapped it, and tossed it into the fire. The grasshopper was toasted on the end of a stick and divided between the boys.*

*"Enyue [You], your cows are eating my maize," shouted an old man waving a shepherd's cane at the boys.*

*This was trouble, real trouble. Their father would have to pay a fine—maybe a whole basket of maize and a chicken, for that old man would surely take their father to court.*

*They knew the penalty and could feel the stick now across their backs. There would be no sitting down for a day or more when Otinga was finished with them.*

*Anyamba ran quickly and drove the cows back to the valley, while Kitu turned the roasting quail over in the fire.*

*They could hear the old man shrieking and yelling as he announced their misdemeanor to the whole hillside.*

*"Now what will we do?" Anyamba asked.*

*"Let's run to Uncle Alasula. He'll let us stay for a few days until father's anger has passed. He'll forgive us if he has no one to herd the cows."*

*So late that afternoon the two conspirators slipped the cows into the yard and tied them securely before their father returned.*

*They passed the mission on the way to Alasula's house.*

*"There's the white man now. Look, he has two little boys. Let's move closer so we can see their feet," said Nyamba.*

*Both boys came running to meet the herd boys. Smiling and with their hands outstretched to shake hands as they had seen their father do, both said, "Milembe."*

*"Milembe," the boys replied, as they touched hands, cautiously looking down at the shoe-covered feet.*

*Before long the boys began playing together with a few sticks and a round ball they had made from sisal fiber. The fear had gone. The boys like to play and they were quick, too.*

*Soon Mrs. Wilson called the boys for their evening meal.*

*"We must go now, but come tomorrow and play some more with us, won't you?" they asked as they called "Mulindwe [Good-bye; God be with you], to them.*

*"They are just like us. Let's come back again tomorrow to play," said Anyamba.*

*"What about Father? What about our cows? Maybe we had*

better run home and tell father what happened before Omulembani reaches him."

"Yes, we've been punished before. I'd like to come back and play with the boys tomorrow, so let's go home and get it over with," said Anyamba.

# Chapter 8

# Life at Kima

All sorts of strange events took place when the new family came to Kima to live. On one occasion a witch doctor was seen following Mr. Wilson on the path, planting small sticks where he had walked. When asked what he was doing, he replied, "I am planting fetishes on his path so that he will never walk here again. These will kill him or cause him and his family to become so homesick that they will return home. We do not want them here. They will take our land, and then what will we do?"

Day by day Mr. Wilson continued to walk down the path, and nothing happened to him. They began to reason among themselves and said, "His medicine must be stronger than that of the witch doctor."

By October Mr. Anderson had come to help with the building of the house. The work began to move more quickly with the three men now to help.

The surveyor came and surveyed the land. There had been no objections on the part of the Africans. The land would be in the hands of the mission for the next ninety-nine years. Since the land was a curious shape, Mr. Wilson began planting slips from the Uganda bark-cloth tree around the border of the plot. One of those huge trees still stands behind the old mission house today.

The men of the community were becoming interested in work now that the Uganda porters had been dismissed. A schedule had been established with regular hours for the workers. They began at 6:30 A.M. and worked until noon. From 12:00 until 3:00 P.M., they had lunch and lessons for one and a half to two hours daily. From 3:00 until 5:00 P.M. they resumed their work.

Although they were not very eager to learn to read, a few of them showed progress. Several had gone through the sixth chart.

The story has been told about the two workers whom Mr. Wilson sent to Kisumu to buy meat. On the way home from their long trip they were tempted to eat some of the meat, thinking the missionary would not know it. To their great surprise when they returned, Mr. Wilson pulled the scale down and weighed the meat and found quite a bit of it missing. He accosted them about it, showed them the scale and the bill, and explained that it was short.

The next week they were sent again to buy meat and again were tempted to try just a little bit of it. They did not know how to handle the bill, for they knew it could talk or the missionary would not have known.

"Let's put it over there behind that tree," said the first one.

"It must not see us. We will still be able to eat enough now," the other one said as he winked at his friend.

After they washed their hands and mouth in the stream they were crossing, they went over to retrieve the bill.

"You, letter, did you see anything?"

Of course the bill did not reply.

When they returned, they handed the meat and the bill very carefully to the missionary. He again weighed it and, pulling his glasses down over his nose, he said to them, "This is short again."

"Oh, no, *Bwana.* It is all there."

Then he told them how many pounds they had eaten.

From then on the workers were surprised and afraid. That letter had not only the power to see them cut and eat the meat, but it could tell on them.

Years later they realized how foolish they had been to laugh when the missionary wrote "rat tracks" on the board and tried to teach them to read and write. "This was the white man's wisdom," they said as they laughed over the incident many years later.

After five years Mr. Wilson had seen a great many results

from his labors. He had built the mission house that still stands and has been useful, after all these years, housing missionaries. He had built a church with three sides for the people to come to worship in. They had learned their language and had left songs and portions of Scripture for their benefit in their language. The one thing that he was so eager for, was to see them become Christians. Workers could be trained to handle tangible objects over which they obtained a certain amount of skill; but the spiritual things took time. It was not easy for them to reject their superstitions, their fear of the dead ancestors, the witchcraft, and the other forces of evil that held a tenacious power over them. He was disappointed because he did not see one Christian.

Nevertheless, through Mr. and Mrs. Wilson's vision, a foundation was laid that has far exceeded their hopes or prayers. We look at the African church as a product of their early efforts, and we see the transformation of the people's lives into polished men and women who now lead their own people. They stand shoulder to shoulder with men and women from every corner of the earth as equals.

Kima received its name from Mrs. Wilson's nickname. In Olunyore it means "well." This was Mr. Wilson's prayer for Kima and it has truly been answered:

May our place always be Kima,
Always alive, always in
a state of health,
Never in decay.
May *fitsanga* [dying]
Never be said of Kima.

Paul wrote in 1 Corinthians 3:6, "I have planted, Apollos watered, and God gave the increase." This truly can be said of his faithful servants, the Robert Wilsons.

# Chapter 9

# The Mission Reaches Out

When Mr. Wilson was compelled to leave Kima in 1910 because of a heat stroke, Mr. Richardson, who had come from Australia three years before to be his assistant, took charge of the mission. The work prospered under his guidance. A new outstation had been started at Ebudongoi (Emusire) and several Swedish missionaries went there to live. One grave still reminds us of the efforts of those early missionaries. Later this station was closed and exchanged for the Ingotse mission because of its closeness to the Kima station. In 1966 a secondary school was built at Emusire by Richard Woodsome.

After coming to the mission, Mr. Richardson married. Prior to his coming he had had a great influence upon the children and the young people of the tribe. He became one of them in the afternoons as he entered into their play and their sports. After they played their games together, he proclaimed the message of Jesus Christ to them. The children loved to follow him to the hills where he prepared picnics for them among the rocks. He showed his love for them in beautiful ways of helpfulness, by purchasing bolts of cloth and then letting them work for six days to obtain enough for a pair of trousers to cover their bodies.

All Mr. Richardson's kindness and thoughtfulness won their affections, and by 1911 he was able to baptize the first two converts, Yohanna Owenga and Matayo Sikalo. In 1912 a second baptismal service was held in which Jairo Opetsi, Yusuf Okwemba, Stephano Kheyabala, and a girl named Mariamu Atetwe were baptized. These were followed by Phoebe Muchilwa, who was the first woman to break the taboo against eating chicken at a public feast. Later she gave birth to a large family, proving that women could still bear children after eating chicken. It took courage, but she broke one of the first pagan links.

The people loved the Richardsons. Mr. Richardson's native name was *Ndeta*. When the time came for them to go on furlough, the mission called the H. C. Kramers to take charge of the work during their absence.

When Mr. Richardson returned to Kima in 1914 from furlough, he began to look for a new location farther west in the region of the Congo. Several men, both African and white, undertook the journey together. The party was stricken with blackwater fever and malaria. Mr. Richardson, Johanna Owenga, and another African died and were buried there.

It was a very sad occasion when Mrs. Richardson returned from furlough to find that her husband had died and was buried somewhere in the Congo. The two Bunyore men did not return home for a long time. Stephano Kheyabala and Petero Minya returned after a long, long time of wandering about, trying to find their way back to Bunyore again. Stephano remained in fairly good health and was still able to serve the church for many years afterward, but Petero suffered brain damage from the high fever he experienced on the trip. Through the kindness of Mr. LaFont, Petero was given simple work to do, such as cutting wood, to earn a livelihood in his older days.

# Chapter 10

# Early Days of Education

From the time of the first missionaries, the Wilsons, education was of utmost importance. Robert began with reading charts and writing on the chalkboard. Mr. Baker's concern when he sent the first missionary was primarily to preach the gospel, but next he wanted the people to be able to read their Bibles, write letters, and do arithmetic so they could count money and not be cheated.

Hence the importance of the schools. Each missionary contributed to the education of the Africans. The major problem for the missionary in this particular era was to establish a written language that involved their learning the language directly from the people rather than from an organized vocabulary.

Atetwi stood day by day with her dark-skinned friends and watched the white people from afar. They were a curiosity and everything they did was observed and discussed around the fire at night. Atetwi lived near the mission and after seeing a few of the boys begin to read, she took more courage and moved nearer. She was an intelligent young girl and was soon able to read the charts of "ba, be, bi, bo, bu."

As time went on, Atetwi began to work for the missionaries.

Her father was subject to all sorts of criticism and ridicule because he let his child work for the white people. This did not worry Atetwi. She was learning many strange things that most of her people never knew before. She became a Christian and was the first African woman to be baptized. Standing with seven of the men and boys, she declared her testimony before her people in the second baptismal class and was immersed by Mr. Richardson. After she was baptized she took the name of Mariamu. She went about the village with the early Christians witnessing to her new faith and was often persecuted, but in spite of that, she continued to proclaim the gospel message.

Mariamu soon became the first African teacher. Although her knowledge was limited, she was able to teach what she had heard to the beginners. The amount of respect they have had for their first teacher can never be expressed in words.

Mrs. Kramer and Mabel Baker nurtured and taught these early teachers and gave them sufficient training to continue moving ahead of their pupils. Finally they were able to complete a fourth-grade pass for certification. Upon this the out school received a government subsidy and became known as a *B* school.

# Chapter 11

# The Kramers

W hen Mr. Richardson had gone on furlough, the responsibilities of the mission were turned over to Mr. H. C. Kramer. Under his leadership, the work advanced greatly. Several Christian villages were built with neatly planned avenues of huts surrounding the church. This soon became the pattern for other villages. Outschool buildings were begun.

In 1923, Mr. Kramer laid the foundation for the Great Church at Kima. By 1927, the year before the Kramers retired from the mission, the walls were about twelve feet above the foundation.

Every rock of the foundation had been carried on the head of a Christian worker. The African leaders felt that the baptismal class should learn their obligation to the church, through service, before baptism. The bricks, too, were made locally and burned in homemade kilns.

From the very beginning, the early missionaries taught and laid the firm groundwork for an indigenous church. The present cathedral was paid for almost entirely by the African church. The building project was completed in fifteen years.

Mrs. Kramer, together with faithful African workers, were used of God to give the Bunyore people the first scripture translated into their language. The Gospel of Mark was translated first; then the Gospel of John. These were printed and

29

published separately by the American Bible Society. Later Mrs. Kramer translated the New Testament and it was later revised and completed by Mabel Baker. Another great contribution Mrs. Kramer made was through teacher training.

Mrs. Kramer began classes with the teachers and trained them in methods of classroom teaching. Soon the government recognized their ability and subsidized several of our schools.

A. W. Baker relates an incident that he encountered upon his arrival in 1914, when he came to Kima with his daughter, Mabel. Mr. Kramer was always eager for a new opportunity to advance the mission and dear Mr. Baker was always ready for a challenge to promote God's work. The story goes as follows:

*A few days after my arrival, a tall, young native, clothed in a long white garment reaching to his feet, arrived, saying that his chief, of the Butsotso tribe, had sent him to ask us to send someone to teach his people. This plea came at an opportune moment, because Mr. Kramer, who was then in charge of the mission, had heard that the native commissioner was at that very time collecting taxes in that vicinity.*

*Mounting our push bikes, we rode off along a native footpath, our visitor trotting alongside as guide, for a distance of some eighteen or twenty miles. When we came to the Yala River, our envoy first carried our bicycles over, returning for me to sit astride of his neck, and then, to my amazement, took Mr. Kramer up in the same way and brought him safely across. It was a severe test, for the river was wide and deep, the stream was strong, and Mr. Kramer weighed some two-hundred pounds or more. We found the commissioner in his tent, and since it was just about lunch time, he gave us permission to consult the headman of the community. After discussion with them, they held a short, private conference and decided to give us a site.*

*To avoid having to ford the river on the way home, we returned by the main road via Mumias, but we were overtaken by a storm and drenched to the skin. The soil soon became slippery, and we had to slither along, pushing our bikes.*

*One tire of mine was punctured, and we hired a bike at an Indian store, leaving mine behind, since he said he had no other solution. Riding wherever it was possible, night overtook us, so we turned into the Kraal of Chief Otieno and had a rest and some prayer and exhortation. We left the bikes with him and reached Kima about 9 P.M., pretty well exhausted.*

The Kramers retired from the mission in 1927.

## Chapter 12

# A. W. Baker and Daughter Mabel Arrive

Mr. A. W. Baker began the Kima Mission in 1905, supporting and carrying its burden until 1922. In 1914 he brought his daughter Mabel there with him. Mr. Baker was certainly impressed by the progress that the mission had made since its establishment. He witnessed the baptism of the third group of Christians. He spoke to Mr. Kramer about the possibility of finding a group who would be willing to take over the mission. The distance from South Africa was great and the South African Compound and Interior Mission consumed a great deal of his time.

The Kramers had been with the Quakers for several years and had served with the South African Compounds Mission in Kenya. They had also been receiving the *Gospel Trumpet* for some time. So during their furlough in Pomona, California, they came in contact with the two Bixler brothers, William and Abram who put them in contact with the Missionary Board. Negotiations were begun. Mr. Baker requested fifteen hundred dollars plus the price of a house for his daughter and another missionary family. But before the contract was completed, he turned the entire mission over to the Church of God Missionary Board without any remuneration. He was very much impressed by what he saw and he felt secure in the transfer.

Mr. Baker has been described by his daughter Alberta in this way [personal communication to Lima Williams]:

*Truly the work in Kenya has grown amazingly from one small and simple beginning. It started because of my father's concern for converts in the mine compounds in Johannesburg who had to return home to areas where there were no missionaries. His legal work took him to Johannesburg and into the compounds so that he saw how spiritually neglected the men were. One said to him, "Umfundisi [teacher], we are like sheep without a shepherd." He sold his practice and went to Johannesburg. He received grants of ground from the mine managers and built simple school rooms with a small living room attached for the African evangelist, who lived there and taught night school to the miners. He himself preached in the open air in the compounds each Sunday using all sorts of visual aids that were ahead of his time. He was chaplain of the jail and saw some outstanding conversions take place there.*

I had asked Mr. Baker's daughter, Alberta, about the Mr. Baker in the film *Gandhi* because many times I had heard her sister, Mabel, speak of their father's association with Gandhi while he was in South Africa. Alberta replied, regarding the Gandhi film,

*Yes, that represented father, but he would have been staggered to see himself with a pipe. He was ardently temperate. The Lord used him wonderfully among the drunk and gambling. I think it was possible that Gandhi accompanied him to Cradock to a convention. No one was willing to accommodate an Indian, but Father's Boer host told him that if he cared o share his bed with him he was welcome, so Gandhi was able to be at the convention. They did correspond for years.*

*Father transmitted to our family a sense of responsibility for other people. I can so clearly remember picnic jaunts in the old Ford with hard-rubber tires, when the plugs needed cleaning, and father would be battling with them. An African would stop alongside and father could give him the gospel. At last he would climb joyfully back in saying, "Mother, the trip's paid for."*

# Chapter 13

# Mabel Baker

The following article will give the reader insights into the personality of Mabel Baker as she relates her early experiences.

*When I came to Bunyore as a missionary, I did not know to what I had come. I had heard that workers were needed very badly, and yet as soon as I got here I began wondering what there was for me to do, and why I couldn't be useful right away. I have forgotten many of my earlier experiences, but I shall never forget how a few days after my arrival I went to Mr. Richardson and said, "You said that workers were needed. What did you mean for them to do?"*

*We were standing outside looking toward the hills to the south of the station, and he, pointing with his hand to these hills, said, "Do you see all those African huts over there?"*

*"Yes," I replied.*

*"Well," Mr. Richardson said, "if you visit those huts, it will help ever so much in the attendance at school." Mr. Richardson went away soon after that. Not long afterward he died of blackwater fever in the Congo.*

*I made the work he had mentioned my special work, and I would go out nearly every afternoon after school at four and visit in their homes. Sometimes it was difficult to get someone to go with me, for the women and girls are especially busy from four o'clock on, getting water and wood and grinding grain for the evening meal.*

*A little lad named Libuka often went with me. He kept me from going astray amongst the little native paths. Even with him, although looking quite brave on the outside, I was often quaking inside, for I never enjoyed the way the people asked if I were a woman or a man. They asked if I were single or married. Then would follow remarks among themselves about how thin I was, whatever did I eat, did I have entrails inside me, and the like. My plan, as a rule, was to get my say in before they got a chance for theirs. Libuka would cleverly understand what I said and then would make my remarks intelligible to them. We usually invited them to the Sunday services. Their usual excuse was that they had no clothes to come, and if we would give them some, then they would gladly come.*

*When I started teaching the girls in the afternoon school, I found that visiting them was indeed the secret of success. At certain times of the year they would pour into a school, but then in a month or two they would be gone again. This would grieve me very much, for I thought that when they tried coming like that, and then gave it up, they would be much harder to induce to come again. So as soon as I began to notice a dropping off, I would try to find out where each one lived and look her up and tell her how much we missed her in school, and sometimes in that way she would come again before she stayed away too long.*

*The girls have such a strong influence upon one another in the sleeping places where they collect to sleep at night. (No girl sleeps at home in the hut of her parents. This is the custom of long ago.) I knew that the reason for the sudden influx sometimes to attend school was because the leader of a certain sleeping place would make up her mind to come to school, and then all the others would follow her, many, perhaps, just out of curiosity. Presently the tug of the old life and its associations would be too strong, and the whole group would give up and go back. If one tried to stick it out she would be the butt of such ridicule that she, too, usually gave it up.*

*My greatest help in the personal work was a woman named Hannah. Her way with the Africans was always so winning that it seemed to disarm suspicion and unfriendliness right from the outset. I came to depend so much on Hannah, that any time when she couldn't come with me it was quite a struggle for me to make myself go without her. Another woman, who would always try to put her own plans aside and get ready to go with me when I asked her, was Salome. I appreciated her, too.*

*This visiting from house to house always seemed to me the most worthwhile at that time for me to do, and yet it wasn't by any means easy. I was shy and sensitive, and the environment was generally repulsive to me; and it was only my great desire to get some response from the people to the glad and glorious message of salvation that made me forget to mind the other things so much. One saw the conditions as they really were in this visiting—the suffering and diseased, the crippled and the aged. The needless suffering inflicted upon little children and babies because of superstition and ignorance is pathetic, and it often made my heart ache.*

*The Bunyore have always given us a respectful hearing. They have never been rude to us when we have been to their homes.*

*I owe much of the inspiration of those early days of personal work in visiting to Mr. Richardson and a very dear invalid friend in England, whose letters I treasured greatly. She wanted to be a missionary herself; but she suffered from tuberculosis. She would assure me in those letters that she loved me and expected great things of me. I just had to try to live up to her hopes of me. She told me once that though an African girl went back into the old ways, there would be a time in her life when her heart would ache, and she would wish that she had stayed in the narrow way. She said that I mustn't harden my heart against such. This helped me such a lot to keep visiting even the seemingly hardened ones. And I proved her words true.*

*One thing I have observed is that many of the girls who were the most difficult to understand and to get any point of contact with as girls, have turned out the most responsive and lovable women when once married and settled down.*

*My home folks prayed for me daily and especially that I would have good health. In this last respect especially, their prayers have been abundantly answered. Whatever of success crowned the labours of those early days, I would share it with my home folks and all other of my dear friends who faithfully held up my hands in prayer.*

# Chapter 14

# Learning the Language

When the early missionaries entered old Kenya Colony, they encountered a tribe with a language heretofore unwritten. Mr. and Mrs. Wilson and Johanna Bila had one advantage: they knew the Zulu language. Since Olunyore was also a Bantu language, there were many similarities. Most Bantu languages share a similar structure, including twelve to twenty noun cases.

An early missionary task was to learn the language as it was spoken by the people and then write it using the English alphabet. The language barrier was a great frustration. We did not know how to translate the simplest choruses. Seeing how playing a little harmonium attracted the attention of the people, they put forth a greater effort to produce a chorus in their language.

Though we did not know their language, nor they ours, they loved music. It was a part of their daily living. Their alliterative language was conducive to music. Funerals, weddings, working in groups, and just ordinary conversations were often carried out in song. As they walked along the paths, a leader would begin a song that the group followed.

A stupendous task lay ahead for the pioneer missionary. Acquiring an adequate vocabulary took patience. It had to be tested out many times before the assurance of its accuracy would be determined. The use of the proper prefixes and suffixes was only earned by skillful practice.

Mrs. Kramer succeeded in translating the Book of Mark and later the Book of John. She translated some of the parables, the Lord's Prayer, and the Beatitudes. One by one, as Mrs. Kramer and Stephano, her loyal and faithful assistant, finished the books, they were printed separately so that the people did not have to wait for the Word of God until the entire New Testament was finished. Later, Mrs. Kramer was relieved of all other work so that she might finish the New Testament. When she and Mr. Kramer retired from Kima in 1927, the Testament had been completed with the exception of Romans, which she did later.

Mabel Baker with the help of Stephano, Daniel Asiachi, and others, spent two years making the spelling uniform and revising it to speak in the idiom of the tribe. It was then sent to the American Bible Society to be printed. A year later, in 1936, the Christians received the New Testament with enthusiasm and joy.

Besides the New Testament, Mabel Baker and her helpers had translated most of the Old Testament stories for the Sunday schools. She prepared Sunday school helps, devotional books, hymns, songs, and most of the readers for the *A* schools. Mrs. Murray and she worked together with the school curriculum which included the beginning readers to grade four in those early days. One of the more advanced readers contained about one hundred stories.

Another great contribution was the translation work and the printing of the Olunyore hymnbook, which contained about three-hundred songs.

In the early days when Mrs. Murray first came to the mission, she operated the small mission press, which was most helpful for both the churches and the schools. The greatest problem was the lack of type. Every time a small section had been printed, the type had to be disassembled before beginning the next page.

Great tribute should be paid to these pioneers in providing the Word of God to these infant Christians. It was done under great handicap. While Mrs. Kramer was translating the New Testament, her young children were often at her side wanting her attention. During this time two of her children died and were buried down under the wild fig tree.

Chapter 15

# Ayub (Job) Libuko Story

## Told by Mabel Baker

*W*hen Ayub, a Bunyore of the Ebusiekwe clan, was working as a headman of a gang of workmen at Maseno, he first heard the gospel. Sisal was planted at Maseno, and several hundred Africans were employed. Since Maseno was only a few miles from his home, Ayub was one of them.

The mission at Kima had been going for some time, but since Ayub was not a Christian, he had not attended the services here and had not heard about the Lord Jesus.

Bishop Willis of the Church Missionary Society at Maseno was in the habit of conducting noon-hour services for the workers out in the open air just after their midday meal, before they resumed their work. Sometimes he preached and sometimes an African would speak, but one day he asked Mr. Richardson from Kima to speak to the workers in Olunyore, for the majority were Bunyore.

Mr. Richardson's subject was Noah and the Flood. His words went home to Ayub's heart, and from that day Ayub began to seek God with his whole heart. He felt that it would

39

*be better for him to give up earning money for the time being, because he wanted to be free to follow the Lord and preach to others.*

*Ayub heard that to be a Christian a man should have only one wife—he had three. His clan was proud of his having three wives; it meant building up their clan. He was a special favorite with his father and very popular in his clan. They looked to him to lead their songs and dances, and when he excelled himself and especially pleased them, they would throw their necklaces of beads upon his head. He was their hero, too, when they went out to fight, for he warded off the enemies' spears so skillfully with his shield that they would just stick into the ground instead of into him, and then he would appropriate these spears for his clan.*

*Imagine, then, what a blow it was to his people when they heard that he had made up his mind to send away two of his wives, and that he was going to take his third wife and go to live at the mission station at Kima. They said he must be crazy, and that he was a very bad man, and they entreated him not to follow the white people's fables; but he said that the more they said to him, the more strength he seemed to get to stick to his decision to follow the Lord.*

*His people then told his remaining wife that if she would refuse absolutely to go with him to the mission station, he would soon give up the words of God, for how could   man get along without a wife! The day he set out for the station with a few little lads carrying his things, and with her carrying an earthenware pot on her head, she went a little way and then stood and refused to go any further. She kept on doing this until he said to her, "Well, you know how I sent my other wives away. I will part with you also if you won't come with me, and I will just follow the Lord without a wife."*

*When they arrived at the mission station, Mr. Richardson questioned them carefully about their motives in coming. He asked them whether they thought they would avoid having to pay taxes if they lived on the station. Also, he wanted to know whether they thought they would not die if they built on the station. Ayub's replies to all these questions made Mr. Richardson feel sure that he was in earnest. He therefore gave him some trees and showed him where to build a house.*

*Being on the station, he attended school and services and learned to read; and one Wednesday in the evening meeting, he made a public confession of his sins and former manner of living. Mr. Richardson and Mr. Kramer were present and prayed for him, and he, too, prayed and felt that the Lord forgave him.*

*He became a splendid personal worker, and each Sunday as well as sometimes through the week he would go with several others to his own district and preach. He persevered in this work until not one hut remained in that whole district at which he had not preached about the Lord Jesus.*

*He was diligent in digging gardens, and would dig in places that others despised, and very soon he became rich (according to the standards then). One day he came across a bird's nest at the foot of a tree. He picked it up and after looking at it carefully, he realized that it belonged to a bird that the Bunyore are very superstitious about. This bird does not build its nest of grass or straw but gets the hairs of a cow's tail and bits of fur or hair of animals' skins to build with. Another perculiarity is that it hides its nest so that it is very difficult to find it. The finding of this nest is supposed to bring good fortune to the finder if he is sure to perform certain sacrificial ceremonies, but if he does not, it will bring him trouble and death. Someone was passing nearby when Ayub found this nest, so he called to him to come and see, and then bade him good bye and told him to keep quiet about it.*

*Ayub then took the nest home and put it in the thatch of the veranda of his house and decided he would not tell everyone about it. Two children had been born to one of the wives from whom he had parted. One had died before he gave her up; the other was a little boy whom the mother took with her when she left Ayub. Very soon Ayub heard that the child was ill, and Mr. Richardson advised him to bring the child to the station. The child died after one week at the station. Ayub and his third wife also had a little daughter. Their next child was a boy, who died when he was eight days old; after that a girl was born who also died just a day old; and in two days more, the mother herself passed away.*

*Ayub now had no wife to look after his little daughter. His father, who had eight wives, said he would be willing to let Ayub's mother (the eldest wife) go to the son who now seemed to have definitely turned his back upon his old home, except that he sometimes returned to preach there. So dear old Ing'wena (meaning crocodile) came and in time sought and found the Lord.*

*After a while Ayub married again, but this wife died, too. Three years later he became engaged. This woman died also. Then all his cattle died. People laughed at him and said, "Did we not tell you not to send away your first wives?" But it seemed to him that the more they mocked him, the stronger he became, and his heart was filled with the love of Jesus. He kept on preaching and preaching until many people came to the services and very soon they wanted outschools started in their own districts.*

*This time he remained six years without a wife, but in the seventh year, he says that the Lord gave him cattle to buy a wife and the wife the Lord gave him bore him five children. She was a widow and brought two of her own with her, so altogether Ayub now had seven children.*

*It is often difficult for a man who has lost several wives to get another one, for people are afraid of him, thinking that in some way he is responsible for their deaths. Surely Ayub must have been very tempted to think, as he saw one after another of his children and wives die, that perhaps he really should have offered the sacrifices prescribed for the finder of the bird's nest. But the Lord kept him true. There are many throughout the tribe who mention Ayub as being the one who was used of God to influence them to follow the Lord. When he died in 1937, he was still faithful."*

As one looks at the village of Essalwa, its orderliness, its strong leaders such as Daniel Asiachi, its excellent school and the strong church with its great outreach, one realizes what one steady Christian can do to influence his clan. Essalwa or Ebusiekwe was the home of Ayub, and from it have come some of the greatest leaders.

Perpetua, Ayub's last wife, was a member of the Bible class that I taught weekly in that village. Her daughter Emma was a student at the Bunyore Girls School and her son Oren taught at the school for a time. The influence of those very early Christians was great and it has been the instrument that has led so many of their friends and clan members into the church because of their faithful witness.

# Chapter 16

# James and Ruth Murray

## (1921-1940)

In 1922, Ruth Fisher was sent to Kenya to teach the missionary children of the Baileys and Kramers. A young Scotchman from the Salvation Army was introduced to Miss Fisher and became enamored of her beautiful red hair and her sunny disposition. Soon the sound of wedding bells livened up the mission.

Ruth and Jim worked hand in hand, alternating their time between Ingotse and Kima, depending upon the need. While the Bailey children were of school age, this young couple lived in a small house at Ingotse and taught them along with the Kramer and Ludwig children. As the need arose the Murrays came to Kima.

Both excelled as teachers and readily found a place in the classroom. However, Ruth was a creative person and soon became useful as a master printer. This she was indeed! The foot-operated hand printing press soon began to turn out Sunday school literature, school books in the vernacular, and other literature so badly needed for the Sunday school, schools, and church. She and Mabel Baker together developed the content of the materials needed. Often Ruth would illustrate the lessons with hand-drawn illustrations. She trained a young man named Angwa. Angwa learned to operate the press in spite of having only one leg, but with the use of a crutch he kept the printing press humming all day long. Through this simple operation the Bunyore songbooks were printed. Angwa set up type and served the mission for many years afterward.

In the absence of a nurse, Ruth Murray cared for the sick who assembled daily at the back door of her printing shop.

This unusually talented woman also taught tailoring to the boys in the boys school. Later she used her skills in teaching many of the women in the villages the new skills of sewing or knitting.

While living at Kima, three children were born to the Murrays but all three died in infancy.

Through the efforts of the Murrays the boys school at Kima was started. They continued to work there until Sidney and Fern Rogers came to the field in 1934. At that time the William Baileys retired, leaving the Ingotse mission without a missionary, and Jim and Ruth went to Ingotse.

Here the work took on a different emphasis, and they soon adjusted to its vigorous program. Of course, the sick were there, too, and Ruth and Jim did what they could for them. The churches were young and widely scattered in this farming area. If anything was to be done, they had to go to the people. With a tent and a very dilapidated car, they packed their safari kit and moved out to meet the needs of the people. They lived in different villages in an attempt to strengthen both the leadership and the congregations. Many of the former Christians were returning to paganism and taking second wives. This became a great burden to the Murrays. The downfall of some of their best leaders was a disappointment.

During one of these safaris Ruth became ill. After arriving home with her temperature extremely high, Jim took her in the middle of the night to the home of Dr. and Mrs. Bond at Kaimosi. Freda Strenger had arrived on the mission by this time and went to nurse her, but Ruth succumbed to typhoid fever after an illness of six weeks. She was buried under the wild fig tree next to her infant children.

This was a hard blow to Jim, who now was left alone at Ingotse to carry the entire load of the mission. His only comfort was that of little Elijah, whom he and Ruth had taken as a small baby. Elijah would climb up on his lap in the evenings when the day's work ceased, to comfort him. Jim buried himself in teaching in the mission school and pastoring the little church at the Ingotse mission. Trying not to neglect the pastors and the outschools, he made frequent visits there.

But World War II began and, being a loyal British subject, he at one time asked to be released from mission duties to aid in the war effort. But since personnel was extremely limited and no replacements were available for the Ingotse mission, he chose to remain.

In 1940, Jim brought his exhibition down from the Ingotse primary school to the annual school show held at Essalwa school. He won first prize for his work. He left the Kima mission early without eating breakfast, to display the articles that his students had made. It was a cold rainy day. The food that was usually served earlier should have been very substantial, but the fare was merely a cup of tea that day. How Jim enjoyed the tea. He left us about four o'clock and traveled home through the rain. Sometime during the night he became very ill but was able before losing consciousness to send a runner to Kakamega to the district commissioner's office to ask for help.

On hearing about it, Homer Bailey went immediately to bring Freda Strenger from Kima. She remained with him until he finally died from blackwater fever. The next evening James T. Murray was buried with his little family under the tree at the corner of the mission.

The world would say, "What a loss," but to the Murray family, it was a happy reunion, the end of a job well done.

# Part Two:
# South African Compounds and Interior Mission Is Given to the Church of God

## Chapter 17

# The Church of God Assumes Leadership

### (As Told by Samuel Joiner)

*In 1912, at the Anderson Camp Meeting, the Missionary Board directed me to go to Africa to find a location for a mission. Our plans were hindered by World War I, and it was not until 1921 that we heard of A. W. Baker, who had a mission up on the equator in what was then known as Kenya Colony, British East Africa. We learned that they wished to sell the mission property to some truly evangelical church group.*

*After a tour of the Holy Land that summer, I took ship at Port Said, Egypt, for Mombasa. Brother W. J. Bailey met me in Nairobi. After a few days with his family in Kijabe and a hunting trip in the wilds of Kikuyu, we took the narrow-gauge railway train for Kisumu on Lake Victoria. The next morning, October 27, 1921, we set out with four porters for the twenty-three mile walk to Bunyore and the Kima station. About sundown, tired and hungry, we arrived at the mission where we met Mr. and Mrs. Keller, who were in charge at the time.*

The property consisted of thirty-nine acres with a few buildings. It was available as a freehold lease for ninety-nine years to the South Africa Compounds and Interior Mission of which A. W. Baker was director. On November 14, Mr. Bailey and I set out for Johannesburg, South Africa, to meet Mr. Baker. He welcomed us warmly and we visited until a late hour, discussing the transfer of the mission and our theology. The next morning Mr. Baker signed the legal papers of transfer, in the name of the Lord, to the Church of God Missionary Board—free of charge.

We were now ready to start for our homes, Mr. Bailey for Kijabe, and I for Anderson, Indiana, by way of Cape Town and South Hampton, England. When I mentioned South Hampton, Mr. Baker asked if we had the time to listen to an experience he had had at that seaport in England. We assured him we were most happy to listen.

"In April of 1912," Mr. Baker began, "I booked passage to New York on the maiden voyage of the S. S. Titanic. The cabin steward had taken my luggage to the stateroom. I was about to enter when suddenly the Lord said to me, 'This ship will never reach America.' At once I ordered my baggage taken back to the customs office. When I told the officer what had happened, he replied, 'This ship is unsinkable.'

"I went ashore and changed my booking to another ship due to sail three days later. On the day this ship set sail, word came that the Titanic had struck an iceberg and was sinking."

Saying good-bye, Mr. Baker remarked, "The Lord still leads me."

## Chapter 18

# Twyla Ludwig

When Twyla Ludwig felt the call of God to go to Africa, nothing less would satisfy her. It was an obsession. Every effort in her life was arranged in that direction. Her home, family, and security were certainly all dedicated to God. Time and time again she dedicated her husband, John; but being of a more practical mind, he enjoyed the security of possessions and was not easily persuaded. Eventually he became a Christian and caught the enthusiasm of his short, energetic little wife who was to change the direction of the infant church in Africa.

They sold their farm in Illinois and went to Bible school to begin their preparation. John took a pastorate to get experience. When they finished training at Anderson Bible Training School, they entered the National Bible Institute in New York City to study a medical course for missionaries. Christian doctors, dentists, nurses, and other interested personnel cooperated with local hospitals and clinics to compile a valid course of study in one year of intensive work. Mr. Ludwig spent a great deal of his time in an area he felt would be most valuable to him, that of dentistry. After raising their own fares to the field, Mr. and Mrs. Ludwig arrived in Kenya in 1927.

Before they were fully unpacked, the sick began presenting themselves at Mrs. Ludwig's back door. Her enthusiasm certainly did not discourage them. Soon the news spread quickly through the tribe, and she was devoting full time to the sick. They came with illnesses she had neither seen before nor studied. Malaria was ever-present, as were intestinal parasites of every variety, and tropical ulcers. Many hopped on one leg or crawled on their hands and one foot trying to reach the house. Babies came with high temperatures and the rasping cough of pneumonia. Sometimes a woman was carried in who had labored for several days to deliver a baby. Here was the challenge Twyla dreamed of in such overflowing abundance; she wondered how she would ever cope.

"John, I simply must have a place to treat these people. They are sick and need a place to stay," she said to her husband. John pursed his lips and began to think, taking a deep sigh as he walked away. He had seen an old house down at the corner of the mission. It had been used by a relief missionary and was now in disrepair. After finding a key, he unlocked the door. The sun shone through the leaky grass roof and two bats swooped overhead. The mud floor had deep cavities washed out by the rain dripping down on the floor. It would take work, but that is what he had come to do. Driving out the bats and rats and working around the termites, John soon had the building cleaned. It needed new ceilings and grass to close the holes on the roof.

With an African helper, he started toward the large native market at Luanda to see what was available. It did not take long to find papyrus mats for the ceiling. The greatest problem was that they were of all different sizes. John began walking them off and trying to measure them to fit into the different rooms. Then he asked the mat-maker to stop at the mission on his way home. He gave him a piece of string to show the exact sizes of the mats he needed.

John made another discovery while there. Passing through the market he saw a hawker selling bedsteads made from Osiola branches, an African wood. Knowing that Africans slept on these at home, he placed an order for eleven more hospital beds. A little farther on, he found the banana bark pads used for mattresses. This would soften the beds and make them more comfortable.

"Now with a coat of whitewash, it will shelter those poor sick ones who would never recover if they went home," he muttered to himself.

The women soon told him about a certain gully where he could find the white clay used to whiten their huts. Soon the sick would have a place to recuperate. It was too good to be true.

"Now the floors; what do we do about them?" he asked someone standing by.

"That is no great problem," they assured him. "We know how to do the floors. First, let us dig up the floor; then we will show you how it is done."

Three or four of the church women came and dug the hard floor as they would dig a garden. The next day they brought their homemade mallets, soaked the ground well with several pots of water, and began pounding the floor, never missing a spot. They repeated the process the next week, pouring pot after pot of water on the floor and beating it until the cracks had vanished from the mud.

Several weeks later, after pounding several times, Twyla asked if it wasn't finished yet, anxiously wringing her hands. "No, not yet," they said. "Maybe three more times! These cracks must disappear or the ants will come up through. It will be finished soon." They said this in a most comforting manner!

Only one of the promised beds appeared after several weeks of waiting. "We simply must have these beds. Where will the people sleep?" Twyla asked impatiently. The mats had not come either, so John went again to the Luanda market on market day to make inquiry.

"Where are my mats?" he asked the vendor.

"Oh, I'll bring them later. My wife did not have time to cut the reed. We'll do it soon," he replied, smiling and showing a beautiful set of white teeth. Who could be offended at him? Surely he was a Christian, for he had such a nice face.

Instead of leaving, John bought all the mats the man had and told him to make more. He found a Luo man nearby who had some others, so with the truck filled with mats, he learned his first lesson on Eastern punctuality. He found two more beds at the market and bought both of them. Now he had enough mats. They certainly did not match, but they would cover the ceiling of one room at least—a beginning! The women kept pounding for weeks until the floor became as hard as cement. There was not one tiny crack for even the smallest ant to peek through.

"Is it ready yet?" asked exasperated Twyla.

"Not yet. Tomorrow we will smear it with *esingo* [cow dung]."

"No, no," Twyla exclaimed. "This is a hospital. That will bring germs."

"You don't understand. We have jigger fleas and they will not live where there is *esingo*. We must do it, for so many of the children who come here have jigger fleas in their feet, and everyone will get them."

"But I am not sure. I think there must be another way."

"You'll see, mama, just wait. The floors must be done every week to keep the jiggers down."

"Every week!" Twyla cried out. "What will we do with the patients?"

That night at the supper table they discussed the day. "Will we ever get any work done with so many delays?" John asked. "I once read an old adage, 'Here lies the man who tried to hurry the East.' Let's try to keep that off our tombstone."

The jigger flea is a very tiny creature, almost invisible, that burrows into the toe just under the corner of the nail. If undetected (the toe should itch) it will grow as large as a pea inside a small sack with hundreds of small eggs. If not removed before the sack ruptures, the entire toe becomes infected. The eggs hatch, making more jiggers. Africans learn at an early age to remove them with a large safety pin or the thorn from a tree. Orphan children or those from careless homes have had such severe infections that they walk on their heels and drop eggs everywhere and may even lose a toe.

"John, my toe itches something terrible. I want you to look at it," Twyla said as she undressed for bed. So putting the kerosene lantern as near as he could, he began probing around. Thinking it was an infection, he broke the skin. A strange-looking mass poured out of the toe, leaving a cavity as large as a pea. As they examined it closely, they found a mass of tiny eggs. A new African discovery—jigger fleas. Twyla was unable to wear a shoe again for several days.

Twyla was in for more work than she had ever seen or prepared for. The unpacked bandages had to be found among the packing cases. But what would the small box of bandages do among so many ulcers?

Jairo Asila, a young man who knew English, came to help in the medical work and she proceeded to teach him what she had learned. Eventually her servant, Mrs. Neva Asila, joined her in the hospital work, also.

The hospital was filled. This was the beginning of an evangelistic campaign greater than a revival. Here was where the gospel talked. Twyla prayed for and preached to them as she ministered to their sick bodies. She had to have help. The patients had beds but now they needed blankets badly. They slept by the fire at night in their homes, without windows in the huts. This kept them fairly warm in spite of the smoke-filled room. Appeals were soon sent to the homeland for help. With no air mail, an answer could not be expected from the ordinary boat mail in less than four to five months and then only if the recipient was punctual in his or her reply. The mission slogan was "Patience, patience. Give me patience, Lord."

Through the hospital experiences, Twyla soon became aware of what the needs of the Africans were. She had seen the results of the witch doctor, the soothsayer, and all manner of other enemies of Christianity. She saw the superstitions and the taboos that prevented women from having nourishing food. Only men ate eggs and chickens. Many other nourishing foods needed by the anemic woman were taboo. Women were the burden-bearers. They did the hard work in the gardens, carried the water, ground the meal between two rocks, bore a child every eighteen months or more frequently, and generally provided a comfortable life for the men.

On one occasion a patient was brought to the hospital after being stabbed in the chest by her husband during a quarrel. A part of her lung was protruding outside her body. Not knowing what to do, Twyla prayed first and then tried to cleanse the protruding portion of the lung. Clipping it off, she pushed the remainder back into the chest cavity. Then she began to work on the husband. She really lectured him and threatened to report him to the authorities, but she softened a bit when the idea came to her about taboos.

"I want you to get a chicken and cook it for your wife. She must have chicken broth," demanded Twyla.

*"Tawe* [no]. That is not our custom. If a woman eats chicken she will not bear any more children," he replied.

"Go and bring it at once. Cook it well so that your wife has the rich broth she needs," Twyla said as she walked out of the room, adding, "Your wife may even yet die and you will be responsible for her death."

The next day he returned with a bowl of chicken and broth. He also brought some of the millet *obusuma* [bread] given only on very special occasions such as the birth of a son. Twyla didn't know who cooked it. Whoever did broke a local taboo. God intervened for the patient, for she recovered and eventually left the hospital.

The most important issue at that time was felt to be to instill into the minds of the people the importance of health care. The time had arrived when the superstitions, cuttings, sacrifices to dead ancestors, and the withdrawal from the potent medicines of the witch doctor were coming to an end.

The people continued to come to the new hospital, but there were not nearly enough beds. By placing the patients with heads and feet in opposite directions, two fitted very well into the small space allowed on each bed. Mothers came for treatment carrying small babies with all sorts of infections from burns, scabies, ulcers, or cuts that had been treated by the witch doctors.

Each patient had dual problems, especially if he or she had been treated by the witch doctor first. The large puncture wound on a man's chest indicated that the lungs had been pierced to withdraw the fluid that was causing him to cough. On and on it went. Sometimes in complete exasperation the missionary would turn her back from the putrid stench long enough to settle her stomach before she was able to carry on. And many times even the thoughts of it at the dinner table caused her to push aside her plate.

At one time the infant mortality rate for babies in this area was 90 percent. The death rate for mothers was exceedingly high also, for they had little care. Gradually they began to come with their most abnormal cases to be helped during deliveries. The old kitchen behind the hospital became a delivery room. As confidence grew, enough women began coming that a ward was needed to house them away from the sick people.

When the government doctor came by, he saw the efforts being put forth for the care of mothers and children and he gave a grant sufficient to build a small maternity ward that housed six patients and had a small but adequate delivery room. That freed the old kitchen delivery room behind the hospital to become a much-needed dispensary.

When Freda Strenger arrived in 1935, Mrs. Ludwig was free to launch her next project—the Bunyore Girls School. Seeing the neglect caused by the ignorance she had met during the short time in the hospital, she realized that the need for education of women was a priority. In spite of handicaps and lack of money, she worked until her dream finally became a reality. Twyla persevered through the years, developing a solid block of classrooms, domestic science units, chapel, and a block of dormitories for women. She changed their entire outlook and young women who otherwise may never have had an opportunity are filling places beside the leading men of the country as teachers, social workers, and leaders in every phase of professional service. What she called the New Africa has materialized in our own lifetime.

# Chapter 19

# John Ludwig

After the H. G. Kramers left Kenya Colony, John Ludwig became secretary of the mission. He also became chairperson of the native *Baraza* [assembly for the African church]. The *Baraza* consisted of the elders of the different districts of the churches. This followed an ancient African pattern. According to C. R. Bell, writing in *East African Background* one old and respected man was recognized as the council leader, someone known for his general ability, knowledge of tribal laws, and wealth. The poor expected him to be generous with food and drink. These elders gave strength and leadership to the new African church. It was no small honor for them to ask Mr. Ludwig to chair their meeting.

Because we often sat in the *baraza* with these men while they began to solve the very difficult problems, we greatly respected their innate wisdom. They were fair to the last degree. Principle was part of their standard. Many people think that because a person comes from a primitive tribe that the person is ignorant, uncouth, and evil. Some of the most gracious people I have ever seen and worked with have been these African Christians.

Daudi Otieno, Daniel Asiachi, Enoch Olando, Paulo Maowa, Kalebu Ottichilo, William Omakhanga, Festo Oyatsi, Willie Otundo, and many others helped the missionaries so much at Kima during the early days. Daudi Otieno was always at every missionary's beck and call. No matter what the situation or which department appealed to him for help, Daudi was there and had the insight and power to help.

To this group of elders Mr. Kramer and Mr. Ludwig came. The elders were strong men of power in their communities and every one of them seemed to fit into Mr. Bell's category.

When a church building was begun they called Mr. Ludwig to measure it and set the stakes for it. He provided knowledge of building both for the schools and the churches. At one time he provided training classes for the ministers. He taught manual arts in the Kima Boys School, but the demands for buildings and the duties relevant to being secretary of the mission and the African Assembly called him into other lines of God's work.

The church at Kima that had been started by Mr. Kramer in 1923 was still unfinished. It was finished seventeen years later by Mr. Ludwig, who completed it from the twelve-foot level above the foundation. Seventeen years is a long time to build a building by Western standards, but Africans avoid mortgages. Instead of going into debt, they set a sum aside each year for the building and continue to do so until it has been completed. Often their village churches take eighteen years to complete.

Much time and work was required to build the cathedral at Kima. It was a mammoth task. Every stone in the foundation was carried on the head of a member of the baptismal class. The church elder who taught the class saw to it that they learned the full responsibility of being a Christian. This meant not how much the church will give you, but what you are willing to put into it.

I am sure the bricks were carried from the homemade kiln in the same way. With the exception of one outside donation the entire building was paid for by the African church.

The cathedral required 114 windows and 5 entrance doors. The building was 130 feet long, 80 feet wide, 42½ feet high with 8,420 square feet of floor space and seating capacity of 2,000. Mr. Ludwig's son-in-law, Francis Paul, laid the brick for some of the upper part of the church. The African church brought in $10,000 through Easter offerings for the costs of the building.

The strength of the Kenyan church stems from the fact that it was a self-reliant church from the early years of its development. The early missionaries attempted to train the church for local leadership. Time prevents me from mentioning all the work Mr. Ludwig did during his twenty years on the mission. He was excellent in giving counsel to the African pastors. He was also a good builder, as the cathedral bears witness.

# Chapter 20

# Kima Boys School

The James Murrays made a great contribution to education in the African church. With the help of Mabel Baker and a few others, they began the boys school at Kima in 1923. As the boys school grew, a qualified principal was needed. In 1934 Sidney and Fern Rogers came to fill this position at the school. Fern Ludwig Rogers was the older daughter of John and Twyla Ludwig. The school had grown steadily under the leadership of the Murrays and their teachers.

Intermediate schools were still at a premium, and the opportunity to attend a preparatory school for secondary education was greatly limited. Many boys came from the Mt. Elgon area, about 150 miles north of Kima, and from the Nyakatch area, sixty miles south of the mission, to try to gain entrance to the school.

How well I remember Mr. Rogers calling my attention to a young lad who had walked for five days to come to school but who did not have his entrance fees. Upon asking the boys how they managed to make such a long journey, they said they carried a little food with them and slept in the bush at night. In those days there was almost no transportation other than walking. I remember seeing a leopard one day as we passed through the Malava forest, through which these boys had walked, so their journey was very dangerous. I do not recall if the young man was able to enter school, but coming without fees was very serious business, for the school had not at this time received any kind of grant from the government, and mission grants had been withdrawn due to the Depression. Great ingenuity was needed to feed, clothe, and provide books, beds, and other supplies for two-hundred boys!

Sidney and Fern were both well-trained and talented teachers. Fern excelled in music and made a great contribution in song and in teaching piano to a few gifted students. She was later instrumental in organizing the annual music festival of the Kenyan primary schools.

In a recent letter Sidney Rogers wrote about those early experiences:

*We had quite a struggle in the early days of the boys school. Very frequently we had to use much of our own allowances to help with the teachers' salaries. American mission schools had a harder time getting government grants than did the British schools. The British officials informed us that we needed more substantial buildings for the boys before grants would be forthcoming. . . . [Despite these shortages] we constructed the first large dormitory. This dorm is now a part of the Kima Theological College. We had . . . 150,000 bricks [prepared] when the Ludwigs returned from furlough.*

Classes were held in the side rooms of the unfinished church at Kima. A large metal building housed the manual arts division. This included tailoring, woodworking, carpentry, arts, and crafts. An open grass-roofed dining room served for meals. The small stone-built church with a grass roof was used for a chapel and the principal's office. The quality of education must have been what attracted so many students, for it certainly was not the physical plant. Mr. Rogers encouraged different tribes to enter the school.

One soon learns on the mission field that he or she can expect anything to happen. Between three and four o'clock one morning, some of us were awakened by the crackling noise of a fire. Rushing out and calling to the others, we saw the grass roof on the church chapel in flames. By the time we had arrived on the scene, the roof had fallen in. Frantically, Mr. Rogers tried to enter his office to retrieve his records, cash, and personal effects. He was desperate. His only typewriter, school supplies, and all the valuable possessions that could never be replaced went up in flames within a few moments. The only piano on the mission was charred beyond recognition. All the pews of the church were gone. While we stood lamenting the loss, the culprit entered the Ludwig house and removed the payroll Mr. Ludwig had brought from the bank the day before.

Not too long after that fire, we again rushed out to find the grass roof on Mr. Roger's garage in flames. By quick work we were able to push the car out as the flaming roof collapsed.

Kima was not the only victim. Every mission had been visited in the same manner. A thief would enter to steal personal possessions and set fire to churches, schools, and valuable buildings. Several months later the thief was caught in the Kitosh area, but the property could never be restored.

When the time came to put the rafters on the roof of the huge cathedral, John was much concerned because they had only manual labor to manipulate those large trusses into place on top of those forty-plus feet of brick walls. It was no small achievement. Many prayers ascended to God for the protection of the workers. Finally it was completed. Then came the problem of the cement floor. Knowing the expanse was much too large to pour in one slab, without modern equipment, Mr. Ludwig proceeded to make small tiles of 2 feet by 2 feet. This was a tedious and very time-consuming job, but it was the only way it could have been done to keep the cement from cracking. At last the church was finished.

The girls school was the next project. As it grew, it was in constant need of new buildings and John kept busy adding classrooms, dormitories, and the large domestic science building.

The Ludwigs had a vision and they laid a foundation for the mission at a time when it was greatly needed and appreciated. They took it through the Depression years, often putting in personal funds to carry the already-started projects. As time passed they became very tired, after serving eleven years without a furlough. Twyla needed surgery. They finally went home on their first furlough in 1938. The war prevented them from returning as soon as they may have chosen, and during this time Twyla finished her degree at Anderson College.

After returning, they built their lovely palatial house on the mission. It was very large, with nine bedrooms, large verandas, and plenty of storage. In later years as new missionaries needed more living space, the big house was divided into three adequate apartments. The Ludwigs retired when they had reached mission retirement age. They then started an independent mission near Nairobi where they worked until Twyla died ten years later.

The African Assembly came to the rescue of the school. A lovely brick dormitory was built on the compound for the Kima Boys School in memory of Paulo Mabwe, an elder of the African assembly. Later a second dormitory was built and named for Daudi Otieno, who had served so faithfully as chaplain and teacher in the school.

In 1946, after serving faithfully and diligently for ten years without a furlough, Sidney and Fern Rogers and their children, Bruce, Beverly, Jean, and David, returned to the United States. Jean and David had been born in Kenya and they were leaving one set of grandparents to see the other set at home.

The Africans loved the Rogers, and they had a devoted group of teachers with whom they worked. Each missionary made a definite contribution to the building of a strong African church.

# Chapter 21

# Customs of the People

All of us have heard the exclamation with regard to missions, "Why not leave them as they are? Why change their life pattern? They are happy as they are. They are still satisfied. We have plenty of unchristian people to work with here at home."

Indeed, many of their customs are good and wholly acceptable and would greatly enhance our civilized culture: their courtesy, their generosity, their hospitality, their care for their widows and orphans, their loyalty to their families, and many more of their good qualities that we have long ago lost in our busy materialistic nation.

But many of the customs and mores passed on for generations were extremely harmful and only Christianity could release them from the suffering imposed by numerous early traditions.

**Government**

Before the time when chiefs were appointed by the colonial government, the council was conducted by an elder who became the leader because of his general ability. He was a person who had knowledge of the tribal laws, wisdom, and authority. He was affluent and generous to the poor. He was old enough to be near the deceased spirits so that he would not offend them. He was respected by the clans. The elder was the leader who judged all offenses brought to the *barazzo* [court] held under the big tree where the community of men gathered periodically to argue or defend their issue.

## Crime

Crime was divided into categories. One was a transgression that affected one or a few members of the clan, such as theft, assault, or murder.

Another was serious crime, involving sacrilege, desertion, or violating sacred things. This category included incest, treason, witchcraft, betrayal, treachery, or disloyalty to the tribe, such as marrying outside the tribe. Sacrilege was thought to cause the supernatural forces to punish the entire tribe rather than the individual. The dead ancestors were considered a part of the clan and were sure to bring trouble when angered. At this point the church and the sacrifices offered may come into conflict. Sacrifices were to be offered for certain irregularities, often not caused by any individual. But because of the superstitions traditionally taught to the individuals, a sacrifice was considered necessary, even though they had done no wrong themselves. One of the commonest of these beliefs concerned dreaming of a dead ancestor. The fact that someone was thinking of the person caused him or her to believe that the offended person would require a sacrifice to appease the ancestor's anger.

The birth of twins, being an extraordinary event, also demanded a sacrifice. Failure to do so could offend the spirits enough to send calamity or illness to the entire clan.

During a prolonged illness, after a series of sacrifices had been made with no effect, the *omusalasia* [priest] might suggest the burning of the bones of the offended ancestor. The body would be exhumed and the bones burned.

When hospitals became available, people who still feared the spirits of their dead ancestors would first go through the sacrificial ceremonies. If these failed, in desperation finally one brave person would defy all the traditions and bring the sick one for treatment.

Patients might arrive with a chicken's head tied around the neck; strips of goat hide around the wrists, neck, head or ankles; forty or fifty cuts or gashes along an arm or leg to release bad blood; or a puncture wound in the chest to release the fluid causing the bad cough. Burn cases were often covered with a concoction of fat and rabbit's hair. Such treatments made the missionary's work doubly hard, and in most cases the

Africans left feeling that the missionary's power was limited, for at this point any treatments begun by the missionaries were long and often unavailing.

A mother in labor had to endure many procedures from the African practitioners. In addition she was sometimes given excessive doses of a plant that produced uterine contractions. Many of these cases resulted in death. The plant could have had great medical qualities in preventing prolonged labor if the dosage could have been regulated, but given in uncontrolled quantities when labor was of long duration, it often proved fatal by rupturing the uterus.

Another of their superstitions involved two kinds of magic or voodoo. First, the person would perform a certain ritual act believed to produce a desired result. An example of this would be to plant a kind of stick or twig in the center of the garden in the hope of producing a good crop. Or someone might place another branch at the entrance of the garden to prevent hail or other calamities. Second, a person might avoid particular behaviors called taboos in the belief that this would prevent undesirable events from happening. Thus using the name of a person was taboo, lest the evil spirits hear it. Instead of saying a person's name, the African would refer to the person by a physical characteristic such as the duck (one who waddles as he walks). Another taboo forbad women from eating such foods as chicken, eggs, or milk. To do so was thought to make them unable to bear children. A third type of magic concerned the birth of twins. If a twin died, the mother must always hold a stick in her arm as she nursed the baby in the other arm lest the evil spirits see one had died and come to take the remaining one.

## Religion

Religion is different from magic. While magic involves action, religion involves thought. The spirits of the departed were a very important part of the tribal life. The deceased were considered as much a part of the living as those on earth. They worked in behalf of the living and they had to be kept in a good mental attitude and not be irritated. They might have demanded such sacrifices as the slaughtering of a chicken, goat, or, in great calamities, even a cow.

Sacrifices were performed by the *omusalasia* [priest] at the three sacrificial stones before the house of the elder of the family. The ritual was usually performed by the oldest member of the clan. Some of the sacrifices were made as they looked toward the sun, especially the one called *okhubita*. It was done by chewing up a portion of flour or grain and blowing it onto the chest of the sick victim and then blowing toward the sun. The spirits of the dead ancestors were the mediators between the people and the higher being.

## Witchcraft

Witchcraft is always evil. It involves revenge, power, greed, or maliciousness. The ability to be witches was thought to be handed down from parent to child. It was usually performed by obtaining a part of a person's body or possessions, such as a fingernail, hair, tooth, or anything relevant to a person's personality, to cast a spell over that person.

Some Africans believed so strongly in this that the belief resulted in death. They may have had no desire to live and would give in to the belief that the witch has power over them. They may have died with no evidence of a physical malady, succumbing to the power of suggestion. The witch may have given a man the idea that he had a snake in his stomach. A clever doctor may do a slight of hand trick to remove it, but otherwise the patient might have died of his own desire.

## Tribal Education

The education of the African was in the hands of the father, mother, brother, sister, leader of the sleeping hut, or contemporaries. Certain hard and fast rules of behavior were established by the nurse girl when a child began to talk. Some of the important rules concerned how to address relatives or adults. Inferiors or children never looked a superior in the eye, but they turned their back to the person when given instructions. Every phase of work was done in a prescribed manner. Housekeeping, gardening, chores, and even the herding of cattle and the everyday activities had particular ways of being done. These tasks were assigned to the different members of the family according to sex, age, or membership. For example, a woman would never climb on the roof no matter how many holes there were in it or how badly it leaked. Neither would a man carry water or wood for the fire. The men cut down the brush in the garden, but the women tilled the ground. All members of the clan had to be careful to have proper attitudes toward the spirits of their ancestors lest calamity come upon the entire clan.

## Marriage

Bride price is a guarantee of the stability of the marriage

between two families. It is the compensation in dowry of several cows and perhaps a goat or two, on the part of the groom to the girl's family to repay them for the loss of her services. Polygamy was common and indicated the affluence of the man who was able to have several wives. He and his first wife occupied a large hut in the center of the *kraal*. Each new wife was given her own hut and a garden. The first wife was the overseer of the *kraal*. She gave orders and demanded respect from the other wives. The junior wife was responsible for providing food for her husband when he chose to call, as well as food for each of her offspring.

## Divorce or Elopement

Running away or eloping with a man without a dowry resulted in social stigma. Divorce was uncommon, for that would involve the return of the dowry. However, if a woman was unable to produce a child after several years, or if she was simply uncooperative, defiant, or hostile toward the family, the husband might demand the refund of his cattle and seek a divorce. Usually this was so involved that he would just marry another wife.

If a woman had one child, the husband was not able to divorce her. He usually married a second wife if she did not bear another child.

Incest or infidelity on the part of the wife involved severe penalties. This was an offense to the ancestors.

The wife always lived at the husband's home after the exchange of dowry had transpired and the bride's family was satisfied.

## Intermarriage of Relatives

The Bunyore tribe strictly forbad the intermarriage of relatives. Not until a thorough investigation had been made was the wedding permitted. Even being related through a distant relative would mean canceling the wedding plans and returning the dowry.

## Initiation Customs

The removal of the lower six teeth of the boys and girls of preadolescent age to establish their identity as a member of the Bunyore tribe was not only painful but harmful. The operator used a sharp instrument to dig out the six lower teeth as the child bit firmly on a stick. The child had to show his or her bravery without wincing or uttering a sound as each tooth was removed.

## Tatooing

Before the days of clothing, the young girls went to a skilled old woman to be tatooed. Using a sharp knife, she would cut small triangular wounds and insert the fluid of a plant into the wound. When this healed it left a raised scar about the size of a small fingernail. As many as fifty to one hundred of these scars formed an ornamental design. The girls paid the woman with a small basket of either grain or beans. Some of the operators were real artists. These designs covered the abdomen and the upper parts of their chests bilaterally, forming a very attractive design resembling a double fountain. Those who were more conscious of beauty and less sensitive had a double row across their forehead and down on their cheeks. Feminine vanity was still in fashion even when clothing was not.

## Circumcision

Tribal circumcision was of great importance among the early teen-age boys. At this time, they went into isolation and remained with their companions for periods as long as three months and were taught the mores of the tribe or clan. Female circumcision or clitoridectomy was not practiced among the Bunyore girls but was quite common among the Kisii girls.

These customs give the reader a better idea of some of the problems faced by the early missionaries. Place yourself in the position of the early missionaries by trying to decide how to meet each issue as a Christian leader. Which ones would you accept as Christian and which ones would you teach against? These were their daily life patterns handed down for generations.

## Chapter 22

# Kisa (Mwihila) Mission Begins

### (by Axchie Bolitho)

*"The land is ours,"* the giant warrior shouted, brandishing a cruel knife in Mr. Ludwig's face. *"Our grandfathers lived here, and when they died, we buried their bodies in this very soil with our own hands. This ground has drunk up their blood. Why do you, now, come and disturb us and our grandfathers?"*

*The mob was increasing fast. Angry faces, flashing eyes, knives, spears, and clubs clutched in daring hands surrounded the little group of Christian elders who stood beside the missionaries, whose calm words about the value of schools and healing were swept away by the furor as pebbles are swept from a beach by a tidal wave.*

*A missionary feels desperately helpless many times, but it is doubtful whether Mr. Ludwig and Mr. Rogers ever felt more completely baffled than at this moment set for the surveying of the land for Kisa Station. Insistent calls for a permanent station and a resident missionary had long been coming from the Kisa tribe. The chief had given his consent. The district commissioner, fully persuaded that the Kisa people really wanted the mission, had given permission. The surveyor was at that moment measuring off the land in the presence of a great crowd of approving tribespeople. But not all were in agreement, for there stood Mutu, towering head and shoulders above a gang of fiercely angry people who opposed the sale of the land.*

*Something had to be done, and quickly, but what? Surely, thought Mr. Rogers, there must be some way to inject the calm of Christ's love into this volcano of hate. Love does not know fear. Acting as on a sudden impulse, Mr. Rogers stepped back and focused his camera on Mutu towering there, his long shining knife held high above his head and his face contorted with rage.*

*"Come back here, you!" roared the enraged man at an elder who at that moment started from the circle to assist the surveyor. "Come back here or we'll kill you." The elder came back, trembling for his life.*

*At that instant Mr. Rogers clicked the camera. Mutu had turned his head just in time to see the flick of the shutter. The rage in his countenance gave place to a look of astonishment. His arm fell to his side, and he stepped back into the circle of his followers. Presently the circle broke up and the mob drifted away. The job of surveying went on unhindered.*

*That was in 1934. Today the Kisa church is growing rapidly. Mutu and most of his gang come regularly to the house of God and work ardently for the increase in the tribe of God in the community.*

In 1937 Homer and Vivian Bailey went to work at the Kisa mission station. With his linguistic ability, Homer was able to meet the needs of the village churches. He completed the mission house and made it more livable than it had formerly been. Since he was the first resident missionary, he laid the foundation for those who were to follow.

## Chapter 23

# Freda Strenger

$F$reda Strenger was born in Germany. She became a Christian while in England before the First World War. Upon returning to her home in Germany, her brother became acquainted with the Church of God in Essen, Germany, where she worked for almost two years at the missionary home. After that she took a course in nurse's training. Longing to come to America, she was finally granted permission in 1924. She then took a course in obstetrics in New York City. About two years later she became acquainted with Mrs. Twyla Ludwig, who prayed for her, and she was healed.

While listening to Mrs. Ludwig speak, Freda had a burning desire to go to Africa. In August of 1935, Freda's dream became a reality. The church she attended in North Bergen, New Jersey, helped her dream come true by underwriting her passage and a limited salary. She left to help Mrs. Ludwig with the little hospital at Kima. She was certainly a blessing sent from God, for it released Mrs. Ludwig to work on her next project, the Bunyore Girls School.

Jairo and Neva Asila were assisting at the dispensary and maternity ward of the hospital. By this time Neva had become quite skilled at deliveries, and Jairo, with an adequate knowledge of English, made the work much easier for Freda in the dispensary and the hospital.

Yet in spite of their help, the entire situation was a great cultural shock to her. She had come from a clean, well-organized, modern hospital ward. This facility consisted of an old mud and waddle building, with grass roof, dirt floors coated with a varnish of cow's dung, wooden beds filled with little night inhabitants, no mattresses, and a few remains of the blankets that the people from America had sent. The maternity hospital was in better condition since the government had built and subsidized a small six-bed ward with an adequate delivery room. It had iron beds with real mattesses and sheets.

Although both Jairo and Neva had a good command of the English language, they were not always there to interpret; and no experience is more frustrating than to ask people about their physical ailments through sign language. There simply is no way to give instructions concerning medications to a person who is unable to read, without verbal assistance. Even when given through an interpreter, they seldom were able to understand. If one dose is good, then they assume the entire bottle will heal them sooner. Quinine was administered in liquid form (which was all our free treatments could allow). In severe cases of malaria, extra doses of quinine could immediately send the patient into fatal blackwater fever. The lines of children and even older people were long as they waited to have their tropical ulcers treated. Bandages were often in short supply, and the putrid, stinking bandages had to be soaked, boiled, and washed by Salome, the laundry widow.

Patience was a virtue. People have sometimes said that the missionary is unusual since he or she was called by God. They seem to think a missionary is especially endowed. Forget it! The missionary is a most ordinary human being, needing more of the Holy Spirit than the most tried individual you have come across in any of the church pews.

I remember Freda coming in, just furious. "I spanked a child this morning. Those new quilts I put on the beds yesterday were simply ruined by a little girl. She ripped the pretty patches out of the quilt to patch her old dress." Now I know that all of our sympathies are with the little girl. Yet because of ignorance, the missionary must endure all sorts of frustrations. A patient comes in with one of your hospital towels, already in very short supply, wrapped about her head. How do you as a seasoned Christian cope with it?

Or you may have had a maternity patient, all scrubbed up, ready for delivery, and suddenly during a pain, she jumps off the table and runs outside—as she has always been used to doing—to bear her child on the dirty ground. With the nurse chasing her down and scolding in half English and a few words in the patient's language, which she does not understand, both are defeated. There may be two choices. One is to let her deliver outside and, standing on your head, tie the cord and lead the mother and the dirty newborn into the delivery room to finish the job. Or another is to force her back to the delivery table and repeat the cleansing all over again, preparing her for the next pain.

Did you ever think that the Great Commission could ever include anything like this? It does. Missionaries are not saints, and going to the foreign field does not make them more saintly. Of all the trying situations, it appears that coping with the ignorance, poverty, witchcraft, superstitions, medicine from the witch doctors, dirt and filth, malnutrition, and injustice in the hospital work are the most demanding of a person's spiritual integrity. Yet through this institution most of our leaders in the church found God.

Freda was a good-hearted woman. She was not always in good health, but she would roll out of bed and manage to pick up the old kerosene lantern, and many times she would limp down to the hospital in the wee hours of the morning, when African attendants were off duty, and spend the entire night with the patient waiting for a child to be born. This was most demanding, for when she first came there were no trained assistants to stay with the patient.

On one occasion when the mother died, she took the baby into her own home when there was no other person to look after the little orphan. She kept him until she left the field. His name was Aggrey. After that he returned to his tribe. It probably was a great adjusting period for Aggrey since he had been raised on European food and had acquired a taste for foods not available to the ordinary African.

Freda's brother was a baker, and oftentimes Freda treated us to some rare German delicacies. Passing through Germany after the war, I had the privilege of visiting Freda's family. They were a godly family, and it was a rare privilege to sit and hear her brother tell of his war experiences. He told me that all the houses in his community had been bombed, as I could well see. Yet their home had not been destroyed; it remained intact with all the terror that literally melted the houses across the street from where we sat talking. I was reminded of Psalm 91, which says, "A thousand shall fall at thy side, and ten thousand at thy right hand; but it shall not come nigh thee."

Freda stayed on the mission for eleven years, healing the sick and suffering, often going when she was unable to go, pouring out her life for God and answering his call when she was so badly needed. After returning home, she settled in Columbus, Ohio. Freda continued with her nursing, but her money was still the Lord's. I remember Roy Hoops telling how she helped them during a time of need. She was little known throughout the church since she had served independently of the Missionary Board, but her work on the Kenya Mission will never be forgotten by those she treated and whose lives she saved.

## Chapter 24

# A *Shauri*

## [Court Case]

In Kenya cows mean property, power, prestige, cash flow, and dowry for a bride. Nothing is nearer to the heart of an African than cows. Although the cows produce very little milk in comparison to ours, the people reverence them—almost to the extent that Hindus do. The cows have names and are recognized for their different personalities, and they often sleep in the house with the family. In the daytime, they are herded by little boys, either boys from the immediate family or by one who may be an orphan and does it for his board. In Africa there are no fences and often a herd boy may become distracted by a bird's nest, flying ants, or a neighbor's fruit tree and ignore the cows.

Cows usually like grass, but there is no code that forbids a cow from becoming interested in a neighbor's cornfield or even a person's laundry if it is drying on the grass.

The latter reason brought Omulembani to the principal of the school demanding the release of his cow. One of the school boys left his shirt drying outside the dorm when a herd of unattended cattle wandered too near and one began chewing on the student's shirt.

This presented a problem involving three people, perhaps four, for the herd boy had not controlled the cattle. That was the owner's problem.

The owner of the cow came to the principal asking that his cow be released from the shed in which it was tied up. In a pleading voice he said, "Can't you see that I am a very poor man? Please have mercy on me this time. It will never happen again. The herd boy was lazy. I'll tend to him when I get home."

But the student replied, "Sir, can't you see that I am naked now and need a shirt to go to school? That is the only shirt I own and your cow ate it."

"I have no money to buy myself a shirt, let alone you," the owner cried in a pitiful voice.

"That is your problem," said the boy.

The principal told the man that the boy was right. He would have to replace the boy's shirt.

"But when will I get my cow back? She needs to be milked. My wife will kill me."

"Whenever the boy gets his shirt or the money for a new one, you may take the cow," the principal replied firmly.

The old man went away grumbling, crying about his poverty, and fussing about the herd boy who had not cared for his ten cows that roamed continuously on the mission. He even insinuated that the missionary could not be a Christian if he did not help him get his cow back. But the cow remained tied. All night long it bellowed, keeping everyone awake within hearing distance, but it was not released.

The next morning, before the missionary had arisen, Omulembani was seen standing at his porch quietly waiting.

"*Milembe*," the missionary greeted him, smiling in a very cordial manner.

"*Milembe*," he answered. "I came to bring my cow home; my old woman quarreled with me all night. She said she was homesick for the cow, so she gave me the money for the shirt," he said as he carefully unwrapped the coins he carried in an old tattered piece of cloth. Before passing the money on, he counted it several times to be sure that there had been no mistake.

The cow was untied, the boy smiled, and they all shook hands and went away happy. He knew that he was in the wrong. Africans have a tremendous sense of justice. The missionary handled the case as one of the wise elders would have done. There was no offense. It was just what Omulembani would have done had it been his shirt.

74

**Chapter 25**

# Daudi and Maria Otienos

**R**ev. Daudi Otieno was the son of Chief Otieno, who gave the land to the first missionary, Mr. Robert Wilson, in 1904. Rev. Otieno has been the lifeline of all the missionaries.

Daudi became a Christian in about 1914 when he married Maria. Being a strong man, he was able to withstand the persecution from the clan that would have caused other men to take a second wife and go back to paganism. No African man was considered to have any prestige unless he had sons. But God permitted the example of Maria and Daudi to witness among their relatives who were still following pagan practices.

In speaking to Maria one day while she was waiting for the women to attend the hospital service, I asked her about her conversion. Maria had been faithfully conducting services each week for the patients at the antenatal clinic.

She told me that she had once been saved but had backslidden. Later she renewed her covenant with God before her marriage to Daudi.

"I was married a long time before my first baby came," she told me. It was stillborn. Later God sent me a son. He was a lovely child, but when he was five months old, he died. A little boy followed, but then he died also. The third and fourth boy came and went. Then God gave us a little girl."

Tears filled her eyes and her voice broke as she relived those sorrowful days filled with persecution. She said, "Those were the early days when Christianity in my country was still in its infancy. Then the little girl died also." George was born following the little girl and he survived. Then came Romona (who survived and offered prayer at the World Convention of the Church of God in 1980 in Nairobi). These were followed by three other children.

Throughout those years of sorrow and persecution, God was with Maria and Daudi. They were equipped with the strength to help those who were passing through the same deep waters.

Daudi was one of the first teachers in the Kima Boys School. He soon became the right-hand man of Sidney Rogers when the Rogerses came as new missionaries. Not only did he offer strength at the school, but he became the liason between all the missionaries and Africans. No matter how large or small an issue, Daudi could be called for advice, and he never seemed to tire with helping.

On occasions when the entire church was needed for a meeting, Daudi sent out the word, and the church was filled for the occasion. If stones or building materials locally obtainable were needed, just a word to Daudi meant they were there when needed. He was often left to supervise the building program. Should a problem arise that the missionary did not understand, Daudi was there. He ironed out misunderstandings that might otherwise have caused serious offenses due to a lack of understanding.

Because of his ability and knowledge of his people, Daudi was chosen to instruct the baptismal class of new Christians. Not only did he teach the Bible, but he never hesitated to show them that Christianity was associated with work. Therefore, when they came to class, he instructed them to bring grass for thatching a roof or maybe a rock for the foundation of the hospital building.

After his ordination, he performed the weddings at the Kima church. By the time he had finished with the wedding ceremony, which was not short, both members of the family knew what a Christian home was with the help of God.

Daudi knew Mr. Wilson, the first missionary at Kima, and lived close to him. Here is a report he gave concerning the life of the Wilsons:

*Mr. Robert Wilson was British. He arrived here in 1905, and he was with another missionary named Mr. Willis of the Church Missionary Society. Truly in those days things were hard. Everything had to be carried by porters on their heads from Kisumu here, even all the heavy building materials. It was also difficult in those days to live with the people here, for they were afraid of the Europeans. They called the Europeans wild animals who would eat people.*

*The chief in those days was my father, Chief Otieno. He was very helpful to the missionaries. Later Mr. Wilson and Bishop Willis went to Maragoli. In a little while Mr. Wilson came back by himself to ask for a place to build a mission here.*

*Chief Otieno was agreeable and gave Mr. Wilson a place at Kima in which to live. He continued to be helpful to Mr. Wilson, though he was not a Christian himself. He sent his people to learn to read in the school, but he himself did not become a Christian.*

*Mr. Wilson remained with us for nearly three years and he and Mrs. Wilson went through great hardships. Mr. and Mrs. Wilson worked very hard and lived in temporary huts thatched with grass. When they bought fowls, thieves came and stole them. They had much trouble. Now I still think of Mr. and Mrs. Wilson as being lights in our country, lighting the darkness, for our country was darkness entirely. Through killing one another, witchcraft, and stealing, Satan had bound the country and ruled the bodies and souls of men.*

*Then when Mrs. Wilson was about to give birth to a child, our people said that when a white person was to give birth to a child she would give birth to it in the water. They said that Mrs. Wilson would go to a small river near the mission called* Musitsabe. *They felt that if she gave birth to her child in a house, or just outside, the sickness of a cough would finish off all the people. So each day they listened and asked where she was going to have her child. Some said that she would have her baby in the water and some went near to the water to see when she would be brought there.*

*So it came as a surprise to them to hear that Mrs. Wilson had given birth, and they asked one another where it had been. Some said they didn't know, and others said maybe it was in the house. Then there was great anxiety among them, fearing that now coughs would finish off all the people. However, after listening and watching to see what happened, they gradually got accustomed to Mrs. Wilson, although some of the girls and women were still afraid and ran away when they saw a white person.*

*Soon the men and boys began to get used to Mr. Wilson and his wife. The Wilsons tried very hard to teach the people about Christ, but they left without seeing one person won to Christ.*

**Chapter 26**

# The Great Depression

**W**ith a worldwide depression missionary support from the United States was at a standstill. Salaries were cut straight in half on the field. Little or no funds crossed the mission books for maintenance or operation. The missionaries simply had to make do. Letters to the Missionary Board, with a prompt reply, took at least four to six months by boat mail. Air mail had not yet begun.

Activities in Kenya Colony knew no depression. All the mission phases were advancing. The limited staff was surrounded with people buzzing like a hive of bees, often making demands as painful as bee stings. The churches were growing; there were demands for more education and with that came demands for housing. More sick people flooded the mission for health care. People were everywhere, with very few trained to assume any of the leadership that would have been so helpful to the overworked missionary.

Then the lovely woman Nora Hunter came smiling into the picture, throwing inspiration in every direction, arming the women of the church for battle. She had hope with a vision and faith that women could do anything.

Grateful to have been rescued from a near drowning, she

longed to repay the debt of gratitude to the Egyptian who had rescued her through his quick action. This took the form of intensive missionary support.

The church needed help and God raised up this little, vivacious, white-haired general who was bursting at the seams with enthusiastic fervor to call the women to arms. Where? To their rag bags. Out came the ironing boards as they pressed out the remnants from years gone by. With scissors, needles, and thread, they started. What happy memories as they reminisced over each of those patches—a piece from their first baby's dress, a patch from those blue pants of Johnny's, or a bit of lace from Thelma's Easter dress. Memories accompanied busy fingers as the women met and transformed the patch bag into beautiful articles of commercial value. The coins began to jingle, though not yet in great amounts of folding money. Someone suggested that they could give a penny a day and pray for a missionary at the same time. Recently, the women reported that through this channel more than one million dollars had been garnered for missions.

This little firebrand, who had often read the stories of Carry Nation and promoted her cause, alarmed many of the pastors and caused them to feel very uncomfortable. Their salaries were minimal and to many the unpaid church mortgages caused them many sleepless nights. This money was needed desperately, and now it was leaving the church to go to the mission field. Nora just smiled and kept working. The women kept on sewing until they raised their first budget.

During the early days of the Depression, two missionary families had been sent to the field. In 1934 the Sidney Rogerses with their two children went to Kenya to head up the Kima Boys School, and Lester Crose passed through Anderson on his way to Oklahoma to take his bride, Ruth, back to Egypt.

Through the Student Volunteer Movement, an active college organization, young people were challenged for missions. As they presented themselves to the Missionary Board, they all received the same reply: "We need you but there are no available funds." That did not satisfy the urge they felt when God called them. They had to go.

In response to Twyla Ludwig's appeal, Freda Strenger, from the North Bergen, New Jersey, congregation, went out with the promise of their support in 1935.

Still persevering, Dr. Miller finally said, "If you raise your money to go and your support for a year, the board will gladly send you." In 1936, I sailed for Kenya, and in 1937 Ellen High went to India. To my knowledge, we were the last to go until after World War II.

# Chapter 27

# Training Begins

**M**rs. Ludwig thought all things were possible. So she brought four girls from the girls school for my new class. We had great hopes for the girls and for their training program. Two of these women did more to change the lives of the women than any other person in their tribe. Both were very good students and after getting past the teasing from the members of the boys school, they settled down and did extraordinary work. The boys loved to tease them and say, "We'd never marry you girls. The work you do is only for old women."

Time and time again the girls would come to the house in tears and express their desire to leave. It is not easy to stand against the disapproval of one's peers, especially as a teen-ager. But more is involved than peer pressure; it involved certain taboos. After we would talk and pray together, they would go back to work, sometimes feeling moody and sometimes encouraged that maybe they were useful after all. The women began to appreciate them and often would do nice little things to encourage them.

They learned English and I learned Olunyore as we worked together. We often laughed at one another's mistakes. Yet the experience was good for all of us.

When beginning this course with them I had not yet developed Mrs. Ludwig's hopeful philosophy. Then I found a most helpful textbook. It was written by Sir Albert Cook, one of the pioneer doctors who came to Uganda near the turn of the century to open a hospital in Kampala. He began a training class for African midwives who would be working at many of the outstations in Uganda. He not only taught his nurses, but also prepared a pictorial manual with instructions on every phase of normal as well as abnormal circumstances of childbirth. Post-natal care as well as post-partum care were carefully described.

The infant mortality rate was still very high. Far too many abnormal obstetrical cases were brought into the hospital, only after days of treatments at home that worsened the conditions. In most instances the women lost their babies and in some cases the mothers themselves did not recover.

One young woman lay writhing on the delivery table as her sixth child was born. She had never been able to fondle a living child. This one, too, was stillborn. The father, hearing about his child, rushed into the delivery room. With set mouth and chin, he looked down at his stillborn, premature son. Beads of perspiration poured from his face as his color changed to a darker hue. The crisis was too grave for him to speak. He looked at his wife. It was not a look of compassion, but of accusation. He was a Christian but God alone knew the stigma attached to a woman who could not bear a child. Her pagan relatives were ashamed of her and made her life miserable.

Some two years and two children later, I received a letter from the husband, telling me that his wife had borne another child, and the baby was living but still very weak. Could we come and take her to the hospital? The child was breathing. Armed with hot water bottles, blankets, and an improvised incubator, we rushed as fast as we could over the rough roads and brought both mother and baby to the hospital. Fearing that the hospital would be too cold, I took the baby to my home, but two hours later it died.

The next morning during devotions the mother stood up and poured out her heart to us. "I've been so happy here in the hospital and have only felt love, but when I leave, there will be difficult things ahead for me. Pray that God will give me strength to stand the criticism."

Her burden became the burden of the entire staff. How we prayed for her! And we prayed for her husband, too, for all of his pagan relatives were tormenting him about taking a second wife. None of us likes to be criticized or sneered at. It is injurious to a person's self-image. Day after day he had to face his classroom with a heavy heart. He loved his wife, but how he wished she would bear at least one son to carry on the family name.

We urged her to come to the hospital before her ninth child was born. It, too, followed the course of its other brothers and sisters. Only an hour later, she begged us to dismiss her in order to carry the baby home. She lived four miles from the mission.

"Yes, you may go, but I will take you," I said.

She sat beside me holding the still form of her baby in her lap as we bumped over the road. We approached the house slowly, for we knew the meeting would be a difficult one. We waited. At last the husband appeared. Then the mother-in-law dashed out of the hut, with quivering shoulders, shrieking at the top of her voice, and wailing as she continued her dismal drone. All the while she uttered in monotonous tones a song regarding the cows that her son wasted on her worthless daughter-in-law who couldn't even bear one living child.

The woman stood a long way off like a child who had done some misdemeanor. We were not invited into the house and by all indications I was dismissed. Knowing their customs, I preferred to remain.

She finally went in but sat on the floor in a corner, never letting go of her baby. I knelt with those sorrowing hearts and asked God to give them hope and strength, and then I left. My heart was simply broken for that girl.

When she was pregnant with her tenth child, I urged her to come into the waiting ward so that we could do everything for her before she went into labor. She was with the women for several days and was relaxed and happy. Then labor began. It was not normal, so putting her in the car, we rushed her to a doctor. All night we waited but heard no word from her. Many prayers went up for her. Early in the morning before dawn, a messenger ran on foot to hear the news from the woman. She had borne a son and he was alive and strong. This time she said, "Send me some food. I'm hungry." Food was carried regularly to her.

I went to get her when she was dismissed from the hospital and took her home. This time the front door of the hut was open and people came running from everywhere to welcome her. She walked in and was offered a chair to sit on. Everyone was so happy. She had now become a part of her husband's family. A bride is never considered a part of the husband's family until she bears a child.

Above: Johanna Bila, 1906, early African preacher in Kenya.

Above, right: An African home in 1926.

Ruben Inhatsi Abwenje (Ajub-Job), an early African Christian.

A village Sunday school class, about 1938.

A woman's Bible class at Essalwa

Below: John S. Ludwig and the church elders, 1937.

Ludwig and Wick Dono- hew, 1926.

Above: James and Ruth Murray, missionaries in the 1920s.

Christmas, 1937.

Miss Baker at the left of her house with the woman she usually takes with her when going out into the yards to visit. We would have a very hard time going out alone to visit, for we would soon get so tangled among the paths that we would hardly be able to find the way home. (About 1915.)

Mabel Baker at retirement.

Mabel Baker and her translator Stephano, about 1918.

Kenya WMS giving dishes to the Bible school. Left to right: Lew and Wanda Goodrick, Jewell Hall, Rita Ayanga, Lois Benjamin, Maria Daudi, Irene Engst, Lydia Hansen.

Top, left: Rita Ayanga and husband John as they left to represent Kenya at the Seventy-Fifth World Day of Prayer in Northern Rhodesia. Rita was a national leader of the women's missionary societies in Kenya. 1955.

Below, left: Irene Engst and a missionary society, 1960.

A mail-order missionary society at Nakuru, about 1955.

Kisii dispensary. The Gaulkes and Lima Lehmer in front of the building whose three rooms serve as church, dispensary, and school. Patients are seated in front of the dispensary.

1951, Obed and Miriam Kutera, founders of Ibeno Mission.

The Goodrick family, 1957.

President Kenyatta signing the distinguished visitor's book while Vera Martin, some ministers, and Mrs. Nyamweya look on.

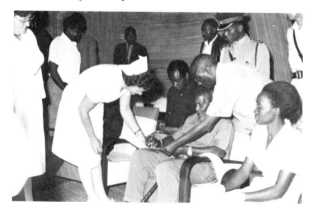

Kisii now has thirty-two churches.

Front view of Nyamwea Maternity Home at Ibeno.

Hezron and Margret Marisia go to Kisii as first missionaries.

Above: Jewell Hall and Jane Engst, 1948.

Above: Nursing and medical staff. Left to right: Hazel McDilda Cage, Merlene Hubert, Vera Martin, Ruth Sanderson, Elsie Gaulke, Lydia Hansen McDonald, David Gaulke, Naomi Sweeny Conrad, David and Joan Livingston, August, 1959.

Below: "Our African wreckers."

# KIMA

The Kima Church

The first nurses at Kima, 1940.

Nurse Freda Strenger, 1935-1945.

Ruth Sanderson, 1946

Kima staff, 1937. John and Twyla Ludwig, Fern L. Rogers, Lima Lehmer, Freda Strenger, Walter Dimli, Sidney Rogers, Homer and Vivian Bailey. (Not present, Mabel Baker, James T. Murray.)

# KIMA THEOLOGICAL COLLEGE

Left: Kima Theological College graduating class of 1970.

Below: Teaching staff of Kima Theological College, 1959.

Missionaries in 1960. Front row, l-r: Kathleen Schwieger, WillaRae Schwieger, Lydia Hansen McDonald, Calvin Brallier, Wick Dononew, Ronald Brown (conference leader), Harley Richardson, James Yutzy, Ruben Schwieger, Jr.

Second row, Donna Smith, Irene Engst, Vivian Phelps, Martha Brallier, Grace Donohew, Joan and Tim Livingston, Wanda Goodrick, Bonnie Richardson, Nora Schwieger.

Third row: Dr. Richard Smith, Lew Goodrick, Edna Thimes, Lima Lehmer Williams, Jane Ryan Betts, Vera Martin, Dr. David Livingstone, Velma Schneider, Glenna Yutzy, Jewell Hall, (not present Sam Betts).

## BUNYORE
### (Robert Wilson began the first mission here in 1905.)

Margaret LaFont
with cooking class
at Bunyore Girls
School

Bunyore Girls
School prayer
room, November
1960; dining hall
in background.
Teachers Velma
Schneider and
Margaret LaFont.

Elder Enoch Olando, fare-
well at Bunyore with Wick
and Grace Donohew,
1962.

# MOMBASA

African leaders plan and prepare.

Dr. LaFont and Edna Thimes in surgery.

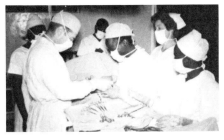

Construction on Chang-amwe Church in Mombasa

Kardatzke Memorial church in Mombasa.

Nora Schwieger and Marita Soulo at WCG convention at Ingotse

Murray Memorial Church at Ingotse

Ruben and Nora Schwieger in front of their Ingotse home, 1967.

## Chapter 28

# Reaching the Needs of the Villages

No condition was worse for an African woman than barren-
ness or the inability to rear children, especially sons, to adult-
hood.

The need for a positive approach was evident. But it would
have to come from the women themselves who followed the
child-bearing customs handed down to them. Another way had
to be found to change the abnormal deliveries into normal
ones by discovering any abnormality before labor began. An
announcement was sent out to all churches, stating that the
maternity hospital would start a prenatal clinic the following
Tuesday and requesting that women be sent in for examinations.

Several came the first week and each week the numbers
increased until sometimes forty came to the Tuesday clinic.
The six-bed ward soon overflowed. We had to send patients
home with one-day-old babies to make room for others.

Daudi Otieno had seen our lack of space and need for a
building. We could always share our problems with Daudi, for
he never turned a deaf ear to them. He was proud of his
mission and every success appeared to bring honor to his
father, who gave the ground for the mission. He could see the

need for more space. But where would the buildings come from during the Depression years?

Then he said, "You say the word and we'll do something about it. We've always built buildings of mud and grass, and that will do until we have something better." My great concern was for the women to have a place to wait for the few days before their babies were due so that they would not be caught during labor with no way to get to the hospital.

*Ndio* is about all he said. *Ndio,* when spoken by Daudi Otieno, meant something was going to happen. The next time I saw him he came with Mika Olubaya and one or two others.

"Measure a building and tell us where it will be put," he said. One of the men on the mission measured an eighteen-by thirty-foot building and placed the stakes for them to begin.

So through the villages they went, cutting a tree here and there, asking church people to donate a tree or a pole for the building. It wasn't too long before the men of the church came and began to build an African building. All day long they worked, and when night came I asked them if they were ready to stop. "No, bring us lanterns; we want to put the rafters on the roof." So we brought as many lanterns as we could find and they worked until Daudi was satisfied that they had done enough.

During the next several weeks the women carried grass for the roof. It took longer, for Daudi insisted that it be the real heavy grass called *tsimuli* that would hold up longer against the heavy rains. In those days they could go almost anywhere and cut grass, but as it became scarcer they were not able to do so. Then came the plastering. Line after line of women went to the spring with their water pots to carry water while others mixed the mud for plastering. The process took many weekly applications for the drying process to insure strong walls. The hospital bought the doors and windows and church men came and put them in for us. It was one of the finest buildings I had ever seen made from local materials. As the women passed the building on their way to and from the market, I often heard them say, "That's our building." And it was theirs to be used by them and their children.

The building was started in April and finished in August. We had invited all the leaders of the different villages to come and enjoy the dedication service with us. They encircled the building with joined hands and put it into the hands of God to be used for their younger mothers.

Soon the women were occupying the beds as they waited for their time to enter the hospital ward for their babies. They brought their food and were able to prepare it locally. The abnormalities became fewer. Others still had had to be carried from the villages, but not in the same proportion as before.

During the evenings we were able to become better acquainted with the women and to know them as persons. Often we sat and visited together. It gave me the opportunity to learn their language and to discover more about their lives and their customs. Each day they had the opportunity of attending the services at the ward, and these were rich experiences for them as they grew in their Christian experiences.

As the nurses advanced in their training and became more familiar with child care and nutrition, they were ready to begin a nursery school in the community. We used the name *clinic,* but the Africans found the pronunciation difficult and always referred to it as *makliniki.* Most of the teachers from the girls school had small children. Miss Strenger's little Aggrey, too, needed day care while Freda worked at the hospital. We began with six children who came and stayed until noon. Many others followed later.

Our equipment was simple. An old hut that was no longer in use was cleaned and whitewashed and it provided a good classroom for them. A few poles with ropes provided swings. The children were used to sitting on the floor, and  so that was not a problem. With a few large tin cans and bits of hide, the drummer made several small drums for the children. We had a band, with flashy hats made from some of those colorful postcard-size patches the women sent out from the States. How they loved to march over the mission with their band leader Frank or Paulo twirling his stick baton. Rita and Sara had them singing songs, playing games, representing all the animals they could ever think of and a few more. Each day they told the children Bible stories. Here the little nurse children could come and bring their babies and play while their little responsibilities slept on a mat that was well-protected from harm. Children could be children.

We insisted that the children bathe every morning and change into their little blue sunsuits. The children loved their baths. If a child was ill, it was taken to the hospital for treatment. Any lesion was cared for immediately. Mrs. Rita Ayanga supervised the clinic for more than twenty years.

Years later I met many of those children, as students at Anderson College or other institutions in the States. Others wore the helmet with the brass lion given to leaders in the Kenya government.

Day-care centers sprang up in many of the villages as the people saw the need for them. At one time we began a few in the more progressive villages and trained their teachers. One of the first priorities for the Kaloleni Center in Nairobi was the day-care center. Mr. Woodsome asked me to come down and give some suggestions when it began. Already more than one hundred were enrolled. Many of their parents were a part of our Kima Nursery School when it first began.

Upon returning to the field in 1966, I found a number of the day-care centers operating in connection with the village churches, under the leadership of one of the village women.

Today the infant mortality rate has fallen due to many factors such as adequate medical care, better nutrition and understanding. It is no longer necessary to produce a child every year or two, and the young families are planned families. Each child is valuable and parents see to it that they receive proper care and become educated. The superstitions have disappeared and the people are following God. Were you to drop into some of the homes after the evening meal, you would see the head of the house pull out the Bible or Testament, read a passage of Scripture, and have prayer with the family.

## Chapter 29

# World War II and Its Effect

When the Ludwigs left for furlough in 1938, they arranged for every phase of their work to be covered. Their daughter, Rosalyn Paul, came down from their farm at Kitale, to be principal of the girls school. The Rogerses were in charge of the Kima Boys School. Mr. Murray was at the Ingotse Mission. The Homer Baileys were at Kisa.

Mr. Ludwig asked the Africans if they would agree for Mabel Baker to assume his work as chairperson and treasurer of the African Assembly. There was certainly no reluctance on their part, for all of them had the greatest confidence in her ability. Her wise guidance would take them through any emergency. At that time Miss Baker was the educational secretary for all the village schools. She managed the bookshop and translated, printed, and supplied material for the Sunday school classes in the villages. She also served as treasurer for the girls school and she always found time to teach a few classes of knitting at the school. Now she became secretary of the mission in Mr. Ludwig's absence. With all these additional activities thrust upon her, she worked industriously to fulfill her obligations.

The work seemed to move along very well with everyone's cooperation. Then the news came through that France had fallen to the Germans in World War II. All the English business people in Kenya Colony became panicky.

Letters came requesting recruits for the government. At one time James Murray, a Scotchman, asked to resign his missionary assignment to help his country in the war effort; however, later he chose to remain at his mission post in Ingotse. We were not alarmed until a letter came from the American consul outlining our course of evacuation should Kenya fall to the Italians, who were now in Somaliland and Abyssinia (Ethiopia), just north of us, moving toward Kenya. If Italy succeeded in taking Kenya, Germany would try to repossess their lost colony, Tanganyika, directly south of us. Our only means of leaving Kenya was to the west. The American consul outlined the course through what was at that time the Belgian Congo to the west coast of the Africa, at Leopoldville, a distance of three thousand miles.

With one privately owned car for a family of five belonging to the Rogers family, three of us were left with no means of escape. We did not have a car; nor did we know how to drive. Mabel Baker and I pooled our resources and then went shopping. We found a Ford station wagon and since we trusted the garage owner, we purchased it. Within a week I had learned to drive it.

We were concerned with the serious problem of what to do about money kept for the African Assembly in the bank, should we need to evacuate on short notice. As treasurer, Mabel Baker decided that the wisest thing to do was to withdraw the money. Then came the problem of security, so she carried it in a stocking money belt and fastened it around her waist until the crisis was over, always fearing that it might be showing. Should it be necessary she would quickly call the African committee and turn the money over to them to be distributed to the local churches. During the few weeks of this emergency, she lived in constant fear of losing the funds.

Prayers were ascending everywhere for our protection and for all the mission work that had been accomplished in Kenya Colony by many different missions. Most of the missionaries and the government well knew that Kenya Colony was not ready for war. Kenya could offer little or no resistance to the Italian army coming in from the north. However, Great Britain's militia had been well trained in army strategy, so by using different insignia on the uniforms of their troops, the Italians were led to believe that the Kenya defense was much stronger than it really was and their army retreated.

By that time reinforcements were sent to Kenya and Tanganyika from South Africa. Many of the German citizens were interned. The mission began to move back to an even keel. Inconveniences and shortages were experienced—more so in Kenya since we were almost entirely dependent on England for imports. Our monthly ration of imported produce was one can a month. At Christmastime I bought a can of jam, only to find that the contents had all crystallized. But we did have sugar, butter, and flour mixed with corn meal. Paper was in short supply. Gasoline was rationed but price always took care of that factor.

Italian prisoners of war were interned in the Gil Gil area in Kenya for the duration. One of the finest roads in Kenya today was laid in that area by the POWs who chiseled cubical blocks out by hand and fitted them into the foundation of the main road to Nairobi—a real Roman road!

Later on these same Italians built a beautiful church along that road sheltered between two mountain ridges, in memory of the days when they were prisoners in Kenya. On one occasion we visited an exhibit the prisoners had on display in Nairobi of a complete ambulance unit outfitted with all the surgical instruments and other equipment necessary to operate it.

The Ludwigs were delayed much longer than they ever expected to be because of the war and they wanted to return by freighter to bring their excessive load of freight with them.

Rosalyn, Mrs. Ludwig's daughter who was left in charge of the girls school, returned home to care for their three-hundred-acre farm at Kitale. Her husband, a Czech, was not an English citizen and was interned for a short time until he satisfied the Kenyan government of his allegiance to Britain. I became temporary principal of the girls school. Rosalyn was able to return later after her husband's release.

All of us longed for the day when the Ludwigs would return from furlough. After more than two years of desperate struggle, we were able to relinquish some of the responsibilities. Overwork began to take its toll on the missionaries.

Homer and Vivian Bailey worked at the Kisa mission. Homer was attempting to finish the floor of the mission house by operating a mill to earn funds. Their children, Jean and David, were born during the war years.

Malaria and dysentery began to be my constant companions. After several admissions to the Kisumu Hospital for treatments, I finally entered the European Hospital in Nairobi for surgery.

During the war years, all imports were cut off from England. As we shopped in Nairobi, the largest city in Kenya, not a single teacup could be found in any of the stores. No stockings were available anywhere in Kenya, neither silk nor cotton; store shelves were bare. The people improvised drinking glasses from bottles by tying an oiled string around a bottle and igniting it. The bottle cracked at the string, and when the bottom section was sanded it could be used for a glass.

In addition to the import shortages and rationing, Kenya experienced eighteen swarms of locusts that year. To see a swarm of locusts fly overhead is unforgettable. A field of corn could literally be devoured in a few minutes if they were permitted to land. The people would go with gunny sacks and baskets to fill with locusts. These were dried and later used as food during the famine produced by the swarm.

Most of the schools were closed because of famine. The drought had been of such long duration that there was no corn. During this time scarcely anything was left to eat. To see the little children with bloated stomachs crying for food is something not forgotten. The women tied a tight cloth or rope about the abdomens to ease hunger pangs. John Ludwig received cassava flour from the government that he cooked into a gruel and served to the people from the large oil drum in which it was cooked. Lines formed of people holding half a gourd to obtain enough for their meal.

The hospital load, too, was very low, for food was scarce in the village, and the families simply could not bring food to the patients. They were always very generous with food and were compelled to share, so it was better for the women to remain at home and get by with home care during their confinements. All the children born in 1943 were called *eskombe*, meaning *cup*. The families could only afford to buy a cup of meal because it was so expensive.

# Chapter 30

# Tropical Diseases

$\mathbf{D}$r. and Mrs. Mack, a visiting Mennonite doctor and his wife from Tanganyika (as it was then known), offered to give us a course in tropical diseases, laboratory techniques, and medications. Several of the nurses from nearby missions joined us in the class. At that time the big house at Kima was unoccupied and there was plenty of room to house the twelve members of the class.

For those of us who have lived alone in a foreign country, it was a delightful experience to associate with other missionaries and exchange ideas and experiences. Missions know no denominational barrier. We are one breed—Christians.

Our working holiday became a spiritual retreat as well. Those times around the big table sharing victories, defeats, discouragements, mistakes, and new ways of correcting them, gave us courage to go back with new vigor. Serving food for such a large group of people for a period of two weeks could have been a problem, but never with a group of missionaries who had a way of organizing and taking turns for each day's activity. An African cook prepared the meals and served them, giving us more time for study.

The news that a doctor was on the mission was circulated quickly by the women at the well, the men at the market place, and perhaps from the pulpit. The doctor was not on regular call since he had come to teach, yet we did call him for serious cases.

Once I tried to stop a mob from carrying off a very sick patient who needed special care. The doctor had seen the patient and had presented his case to the class for study. He explained the extent of the illness and the prognosis as being very serious. The old man was barely conscious. When the people despair for a person's life, the family often comes in a group with a stretcher to carry the patient home to die—as happened on that night.

The mob was noisy. Some wanted the patient to stay at the hospital and others asked that he be taken away immediately. One belligerent young man came up to me demanding the patient's release at once. They were not in any mood for reasoning. Their plans had been made and they intended to carry them out. I tried to explain the dangers of taking their patient home, but the young man came and stood as near me as he could with our chests touching, challenging me. I had stepped back into the dispensary to look at the patient's chart when I heard the door close and the click of the padlock. At first I was infuriated, but as I heard the crowd and their voices move farther and farther away as they walked down the road carrying the patient, I smiled to myself. The joke was on me. I was the prisoner and they were free. Very soon someone missed me and came to my rescue and unlocked the door, so it was not too painful an experience.

The story does not end there. Months later, after holding the service in a village and greeting the different ones at the door, a tiny little old man with a sharp twinkle in his eye took my hand and said, "Do you remember me?"

Not remembering him, I asked, "Have you been a patient at the hospital?"

Then he related the above incident, but added, "God healed me, and now I am well and strong again."

That man was the pastor of the church in his village. Through the African's simple faith, they believed that God was able to do just what he said. The church took over when the hospital could not.

How we rejoice when we hear of incidents such as this. We treat patients, pray for them, and when they leave, others enter into our focus of interest and they may be forgotten. But their problems are not forgotten. If they are Christians, other Christians take up their burden and pray the prayer of faith for them in the church.

## Part Three:
## The Church Takes
## Root and Grows

### Chapter 31

# The African Church
# Advances

With the Depression and World War II behind us and the few missionaries who remained from that era to carry on the work, it was evident that the pioneer stage must be left behind as Kenya Colony looked to future advancement. The early missionaries did an excellent job and certainly worked under great handicaps because of limited personnel and lack of funds and equipment with which to work. Salaries had been cut to the bone; maintenance often had been drastically cut or withdrawn.

After the war, the African people settled down to normal living once more, but with a sense of dissatisfaction. With the growth of the population, the gardens that had been adequate for the smaller families, were unable to provide a living from those small plots of ground that the families had inherited. The young men who inherited land from their fathers found that it had been divided among their brothers until there was scarcely enough left on which to build a small hut. Bunyore became one of the most densely populated areas in North Kavirondo. Education was the only solution if people were to get out of their present dilemma. A missionary once said, "A father will go to jail for his taxes, but his son's school fees must be paid."

The children needed more schools. There were long entrance waiting lists, and many times the boys and girls who were admitted to a school had to walk eight or more miles from home. It meant leaving early and returning home at dark. Unless the schools had been subsidized by the government with qualified teachers, their training had no recognition. Pastors or helpers tried to teach the children at the church, but soon the people began clamoring for more schools.

The Kima Boys School was offered thirty acres of land at the Ingotse Mission. With the limitations of ground at Kima, it seemed advisable to move it there. Upon the retirement of Sidney and Fern Rogers, Ruben and Nora Schwieger came in 1947 from Oklahoma, where Ruben had been a high school principal, to take over the boys school. About six months later they moved the school to Ingotse. Nora had been a domestic science major, but she found herself assuming the role of an unqualified nurse who was forced to treat the many cases waiting at the back door for her each morning. Courageously, she did it.

Mrs. Ludwig, who had begun the girls school and had led it through the darkest stages of its development, was nearing retirement age, and so when Frank and Margaret Lafont came in 1946, they both began to work in the school. When the Ludwigs went on furlough, Magaret LaFont became its principal.

Jewel Hall had come to replace me in 1944, but was now deeply involved in the girls school and the beginning of a teacher training center.

Ruth Sanderson, a registered nurse, had come in 1946 to replace Freda Strenger, who had now retired from the general hospital at Kima. Ruth would gradually work there and then in the maternity hospital.

As the group of missionaries grew, each found a place in which he or she was qualified. Herman and Lavera Smith were the first to come to Kenya in 1946 after the war. Herman acted as Mission Secretary and Lavera, his wife, helped in the girls school by teaching music. She worked with the Sunday school teachers as well. I returned to my former work but saw the need in an untouched field that beckoned me. It was that of teaching Bible to the women in the various villages. Prior to this time, Mabel Baker had worked with the women as time allowed, but her involvement in the translation of the Psalms took most of her time.

Since I had been at the hospital with so many of the women during the birth of their babies, most of them were my friends. The contacts made formerly through our visitations to the villages had proved to be stepping-stones.

In 1947 Irene Engst, a practical nurse from Canada, came to live with Jewell Hall. She soon found a very busy place in caring for the many very ill patients who came to the door for treatment.

The mission was thrust into this transitional era and practically everyone was influenced by it. The demand for departmental heads, who would be responsible for each department, superseded the one missionary head who carried the responsibility for everything. New budgets were made, which each department submitted in advance for approval. Monthly staff meetings were conducted, led by its own elected chairperson and secretary, and problems were approached by a democratic staff.

The staff meetings were cordial. We always met for a potluck lunch in connection with the staff meeting. After the meeting we had a devotional time together. Then since some stayed overnight because of the distance from the mission, we all sat around together and had a happy social time with games, conversation, or any other interests that we shared. If the meeting happened during the school vacation, the missionaries' children enjoyed the fellowship with one another. We became in essence a single, happy family. All the children had "aunts" and "uncles" in abundance. Those children became special favorites of their aunties who lived near them. I had several little cookie kids who knew the exact location of the cookie jar, and I saw to it that there were always a few cookies there for the youngsters.

One of the lessons we as missionaries, as well as missionary boards, have learned is the importance of our missionary's children. Parents dedicate their lives to missions, but the children have little to do with it. In years gone by, when missionaries were few and far apart, with so many pressing tasks to be done, parents sometimes forgot their children and gave all their time trying to save the heathen. All of us have seen the result of that.

Sometimes when our children return home after living in a foreign land, they are different and do not fit into American culture readily. They need to be loved and nurtured, even though they are of college age and away from their parents who remain in a foreign land. With a parent in the States, they can always be reached by telephone, but it is difficult to reach a missionary parent, and so they sometimes feel very frustrated and lonely. The greatest sacrifice of parents who have served in Kenya Colony has not been the lack of modern things, or the sacrifice of material possessions, but having to turn their children over to a boarding school two-hundred miles away from home when they are only six years old. And they miss them at every age. So when they get their vacations (one month after each trimester), the parents are very careful to plan their work in order to do special things with their children.

## Chapter 32

# Jewell Hall Comes to Mwihila

The Mwihila mission had been started in the heart of a jungle, in a deep forest with thick trees and long, tangled, hanging vines. The trees were filled with Calabus monkeys that put on a beautiful show every evening before dusk by swinging back and forth between the trees with their young. Snakes were plentiful.

When Ludwigs left for furlough, Jewell Hall, the new principal of the teacher training center at Mwihila, fell heir to their old sedan. Her classrooms were made of mud and wattle with grass roofs. But she was equal to the challenges. She and I were both trained by Twyla Ludwig, whose theory was that "nothing is too hard for you and God to handle together." Indeed it wasn't, for Jewell plunged in and cut down the bush, mowed the lawn, planted flowers, and pushed back the jungle. But the mats in the house were not very secure and the snakes and bats loved living above her living quarters. Fortunately the house had screen doors.

Jewell related a story to us of one incident when an English government official had come for dinner. They were sitting at the table when a snake crawled up the outside of the screen door. He was shocked, but Jewell in her nonchalant manner said, "Oh, just wait—the bats will soon be coming." About that time two or three bats flew from a gap in the ceiling mats. Whether she received a grant for her teacher training center after that I don't know, but she thoroughly enjoyed the experience. She had a gift for shocking people and enjoying it.

After Jewell had been there nine months, Irene Engst came to assist her. Since they lived and worked together for more than a quarter of a century, I have asked Irene to write about Jewell's work:

*Jewell's first three years were spent at Kima station where she taught in the girls school, assisted with the hospital work, and during the last year taught teacher trainees.*

*Once Jewell became seriously ill with malaria. Mary Jeremiah, her student helper, stayed with her during the long nights of the illness and was instrumental in saving her life.*

*When the decision was made to establish the teacher training center at Mwihila, Jewell moved there to be principal and teacher. Susie and Timothy Litondo had been teaching at Kima and they moved her to Mwihila. Timothy was to teach at the center and Susie in the public school.*

*Two mud and wattle dormitories, a classroom, and a house for the Litondo family had been built for the school. Jewell moved into the unfinished mission house that had been built by the Women of the Church of God in 1937. The missing leg of the old wood stove was propped up with a brick. Cupboards had not yet been added. Water had to be carried from a spring to the bathtub. The mat ceilings and open transoms above the doors allowed bats to move freely from room to room. Kerosene lamps provided light. The house did have a lovely shining red cement floor that was clean and cheery. Screen doors proved to be useful in keeping the snakes outside.*

*Though Jewell had gone to Mwihila to work in the teacher training center, as soon as the people heard that she was there they brought the sick to her house for treatment. Mabel Benjamin came from Kima to assist her in nursing care, and nine months later Irene Engst came.*

*The teacher training center was coeducational, which was rarely heard of at that time. Jewell felt that these boys and girls could study and work together, which proved to be true. About half the class of the twenty-five chosen were girls. They had completed grades six to eight and were trained for a year before being certified to teach fourth grade. The mission supplied the personnel, and the government paid the salaries and maintained the school.*

*Except for some texts, books were in very short supply.*

Chalkboards were used freely as a teaching apparatus, as were such local materials as sticks, stones, seeds, and banana bark. Even though they had little with which to work, the students did learn. Some of these first students became teachers who served for many years. The trainees would study for a period and then do a block of teaching in nearby schools. The teachers would observe them and help them with teaching methods.

Because the school buildings were built on the side of a hill, they had no level space for a physical education field. Jewell enlisted her teachers and students to dig the hill away, leveling it by hand to make a standard-size playing field.

On one of the many walks Jewell took with her students, she came upon a beer drinking party. As she stopped to chat with them, one of the elder men said to her, "You are too late to help us, but maybe you can help our children." This was engraved on Jewell's heart as something she could never forget. Her deep desire was to help the young people. She was intensely interested in her students and very strict with them. They accepted this because they knew she had confidence in their success.

Revivals were held in the school during the year. Some students were Christians when they came and others gave their hearts to the Lord while there. Several of these young people became leaders in the church.

As the faculty increased, the mud buildings were replaced with brick buildings, and more students were admitted. The school was upgraded to T3, which enabled the teachers to teach classes above grade four. Higher qualifications were required, and the course was for two years instead of one. The school moved on to become a high school and additional buildings were added as needed. Faculty housing and a new unit were added.

Reverend Musa Shippira arranged for Jewell to visit the church meetings at Mwihila from time to time. Accompanied by Irene and a teacher or student, Jewell would walk or drive to the villages. People received Christ and the missionaries learned to share their struggles. We always stayed to eat with the Africans, and through the years friendships were formed as we became acquainted with the African culture.

Jewell had a burden for the pastors who had not had the opportunity of formal Bible training. In time weekly classes were started at Mwihila for the Kisa pastors. Lessons were typed and copies made for their study and sermon preparation. Both women taught these classes for a number of years.

*Area meetings were held in the grove near the mission house. People would walk a long way to attend these services, especially at Christmas and Easter. The area chairperson, Musa Shippira, was very active in organizing these meetings and helped to get the necessary land for the mission buildings. Later a brick church replaced the mud and wattle one which was there when Jewell went to Mwihila.*

*Jewell was a real pioneer. Constantly battling malaria, she worked under hardship and earned the respect of the people. Fellow missionaries enjoyed her company. She was full of fun and kept people entertained. She was deeply dedicated to the task before her, loved the people, and desired to do the will of God.*

# Chapter 33

# Bunyore Girls School

Margaret and Frank LaFont came to Kima in 1946. They, too, had been influenced by the Kramers when they dedicated themselves for mission service.

When Mabel Baker returned from furlough nine months later, the LaFonts moved into the old mission house built by Robert Wilson and lived there for the next twenty-seven years. The Ludwigs were now living in their newly built home.

In May 1947, Margaret began teaching full time in the girls school when the Ludwigs left for furlough. She became principal of the school. Frank also taught in the school, but he gradually became involved in other duties around the mission. The outschools wanted to move out of the church buildings into their own schools, and so Frank helped measure the land to build their schools. He said he must have bought hundreds of slates during that time for the children to learn to write.

This was a time for growth and expansion of the mission. The culture was changing and a new emphasis was being put on education. The people of the girls school since the early days had chopped their own firewood, dug their gardens to raise their greens, beans, and bananas; they carried the water for laundry, cooking, and other purposes from the well quite a distance down over the hill—tasks that consumed all their free time. As the population grew, it was no longer possible to go into people's gardens to gather firewood.

Parents were now paying fees for their daughters to receive their education and they exerted pressures on them to apply themselves in order to pass their examinations. The Kenya Primary Education Exams were casting a stigma on the school. Something had to be done to improve the girls' performance if government grants were to be forthcoming. Some provision had to be made to bring water from the community spring and to save the time needed for studies.

The school no longer taught gardening, since foodstuffs could be bought locally, and so several changes were necessary in the budget of the school. Frank set out with several others to obtain a water supply for the school. A worker was hired to cut wood and later a cook took over the food preparation. Bananas, greens, and beans were included in the food budget. Most of these girls would become educated and would no longer be part of the local society but could afford a servant or be able to buy needed foods.

Margaret, determined to prepare the girls to earn higher passing grades on the tests, found it necessary to change the program so that more time could be given to study. The examinations were difficult and many students would be eliminated by low scores if better study habits were not utilized. One must recall that the examinations taken by African children were prepared and graded in England by English standards!

Margaret had to fit her expenses into a budget of forty-three dollars per girl per year. That included food, school supplies, uniforms, two sheets, and two blankets for each of 152 girls. Margaret cut out the 450 uniforms herself and supervised their construction; learning to sew was part of the training. These improvements resulted in better passing grades. Kima Girls School had 100 percent passes for seven years and high averages for other years.

In 1964, four of the Church of God schools, including Bunyore Girls School, became secondary schools. This meant that more science was required. Students studied English, Swahili, biology, physics, health sciences, chemistry, domestic science, history, geography, math, algebra, geometry, secretarial courses, religious knowledge, and the synoptic gospels.

The exams later came to be patterned after the Cambridge exams and all papers formerly done in England were hereafter corrected in Kenya. The Bunyore girls school, a high school now, had 250 students.

In 1968, the school was turned over to an African headmistress. The school property has now been fenced off from the mission and is no longer under mission control but has been governed by a Church of God board of governors. A number of our missionaries have taught in the girls school: Mrs. LaFont; Lavera Smith and Grace Donohew, music; Nora Schwieger, domestic science; Martha Brallier, assistant principal; later Olive Fiscus, Velma Schneider, Esther Beatty, Caroline Upchurch, and others. Velma Schneider became the assistant principal for two terms. A great number of other short-term teachers served during the transition period while Africans were finishing their degrees. Their names will be mentioned in another part of this book.

Since Jewell's passing those who worked with her miss her jovial nature and perseverance through great odds. Her life was filled with many disappointments and yet she rose above them, lifted her head, made a witty remark, and kept her faith secure in God.

Mrs. Revere Cook, lifetime friend of Jewell's, wrote lovingly of her. She expressed the sentiments of every member of the mission staff and all the Africans who loved her so much:

*Jewell possessed varied abilities: she was a loving teacher of youth, an entertaining conversationalist, a competitive game player, a marvelous cook, a devoted church worker, a gracious hostess, a fantastic storyteller, a challenging speaker, a loyal friend—all these and more! Jewell was extraordinary in her wisdom, insight, generosity, and dedication to God's work. However, the one trait that especially endeared Jewell to her many friends was her delightful sense of humor. She relished stories of people predicament, including those about herself.*

*To be a guest in Jewell's home was an unforgettable pleasure. I can hear her yet, telling anecdotes with great gusto, embellished by her hearty laugh. I can see, in my mind's eye, the mischievous twinkle in her eyes. I can sense anew the excitement felt as I listened, sometimes for hours, to her recounting of various African experiences.*

As the church celebrated its centennial year in Anderson in 1980, Jewell lay dying and passed away a few days later. Her monument was not in stone, but in the lives of the men and women who had been trained and saved under her godly influence.

One of the things that gratified Margaret LaFont during the 1983 World Conference of the Church of God was meeting many of her successful students at Nairobi. The principal (at the time of this writing) is Priscilla Were, a former student of Bunyore Girls School when Margaret LaFont was there. She is from Busia and was trained at a university. Now the school has moved up to junior college level and has an enrollment of six-hundred students. Mrs. LaFont remarked about the standard at which the girls school has held itself. Everything was neat, clean, and orderly. Mrs. LaFont's party of thirty-eight visitors to Nairobi was entertained at a splendid tea at the school, and several beautiful choral numbers were sung.

The LaFont children deserve mention. Frank and Margaret always regretted that their work separated them from their children, for they were a very devoted family, but they look back with satisfaction and enjoyment.

During their first year in Kenya, Margaret taught seven-year-old Donald. Pressures of mission duties compelled her to send him to Rift Valley Academy with his brother, Harold. This was two-hundred miles away from home. These separations were extremely hard on a closely knit family. The LaFonts were careful to spend time with their boys during the month's vacation following each school term.

During the Mau Mau insurrection the LaFonts were very fearful of letting Donald remain at the school, which was in the heart of the Mau Mau territory. When they left for their first furlough, they left Harold behind to begin his university training; after their second furlough, Donald remained behind.

Chapter 34

# Building Churches and Institutions

**W**hen Frank and Margaret LaFont came to the mission, they seemed to shed a contagious sense of joyous well-being. When Frank was around, the mission abounded with laughter and cheer, especially when he and Herman Smith met. Their good-natured banter lightened any problem. They were a tonic to serious-minded missionaries. Yet all of them were concerned and conscientious when the need arose. Both Frank and Herman were men of God with a vision for the work.

The first few weeks after their arrival, Frank and his teenage son Harold could be found with paint brushes in their hands, trying to brighten up the dull spots they could find everywhere. Not much had been done during the war because the staff was so limited and other tasks took priority.

Frank and Margaret both began teaching in the girls school, but that did not entirely satisfy them. They were anxious to get into the villages. They began going there for Sunday services. It did not take long for them to see the tremendous need for assistance in the villages. Most of the pastors had little opportunity for training and were doing an excellent job in spite of this lack. But with some guidance, they could do much better.

Frank was given the responsibility of assisting them. This he took very seriously. Prior to this time, no regular Bible teaching had been given to the pastors except from the pulpit. They were glad when Frank was finally able to set up regular classes in the villages. Numerous stations were located throughout the villages for the pastors in nearby villages so that they could attend without too much inconvenience. Refresher courses in pastoral methods and regular Bible studies became a part of the routine.

As they sat around the table after services or classes, they opened their hearts and told Frank their needs. Education was a priority now for the country. The pastor or local helper had been conducting classes for children in the church, offering beginning classes in reading and writing. The children used slates to copy the words from the chalkboard. No other equipment was available. More subsidized schools with properly trained teachers were needed, for unless they studied in the recognized government-supported schools, their learning would be inadequate and valueless. They needed to move out of the churches and have schools built for their purpose in the area. The children who were able to get into the schools did so only after a long period with their names on the waiting lists. Many of the boys and girls had to walk eight or more miles each day to attend school, leaving home early in the morning and returning home after dark in the evening.

As they found suitable plots for the schools, Frank would assist them by measuring the land for the building.

Until schools were established in the villages, the roads to the villages often ended in a footpath that was impassable by car, necessitating that people walked the rest of the way. Roads would usually appear rather quickly after a school had been built.

While this was happening in the villages, Jewell Hall was at Mwihila opening a teacher training facility to supply trained teachers for the new schools. Keeping ahead of their needs was the important job now at hand for a progressing, growing church if they were to attain their goal. The missionary was there to help them do just that. During this period of advancement, the same spirit was felt in the growing church. The people no longer were satisfied with their mud and wattle, grass-roofed churches. They began to speak to the leaders about concrete floors, brick or stone walls, and a permanent roof. As soon as the building had been measured for them, according to the size they needed, they began the work themselves. From the very beginning, they had been taught to develop a self-reliant church. Many times they took as long as eighteen years to finish a church, but it was theirs and it was debt free.

Frank did not come to be a builder, yet when he started, he built for the next twenty years. His first real adventure was the hospital at Mwihila. This all happened as a result of an experience he had one day as he was driving to Mwihila Mission. Passing a group of patients sitting under a tree where Irene Engst was conducting a wayside dispensary, treating the sick, Frank suddenly saw all of the patients running from under the tree. Coming closer, he discovered the reason. Above Irene was a very poisonous spitting viper, coiled around the limb.

## Mwihila Hospital

After this experience and growth of the patient clientele, a larger building was needed. Frank again came to the rescue. In 1948, he began constructing the concrete floor of the first little building that would be followed by the Mwihila Hospital. African women had finished the little mud and wattle ward on the concrete floor Frank laid. Although it was only twenty-four feet square and temporary, it served for about five years until the large hospital had been dedicated. Our missionaries had to adjust to any circumstances, no matter how inconvenient, to spread the gospel message. They were not people who enjoyed living in squalor, but as soon as possible they did all within their power to improve the situation, even when seemingly there were no means to do so.

In 1953 the Women of the Church of God raised seventy-five thousand dollars to build a hospital at the Mwihila Mission. The plan included a modern hospital of 100 beds, housing for two doctors and four nurses, a training school for African nurses, and housing in which they would live. These buildings did not come custom made, but everything came from native elements. Bricks were made from local mud and burned in homemade kilns fired with trees and stumps. To break stone for concrete, they would shatter the large granite boulders, build fires around them, and pour water over them to make them pop. The fragments were then taken and pounded by hand with an iron mallet to the size used in making concrete. All day long men sat in a little shed they had built under a shading grass roof, breaking the rock into small pieces. When they had enough for a load, the mission lorry [truck] came to buy them. The sand that was hauled from the rivers to the mission still needed to be sifted. When the water had been carried in sufficient amounts to begin, they started the stirring process with their hoes and shovels to mix the concrete.

The Church of God has been most fortunate in having excellent builders, not only because of their knowledge of building, but also their ability to produce a beautiful structure with a minimum budget. Some of the builders were H. C. Kramer, J. S. Ludwig, Sidney Rogers, Herman Smith, Frank LaFont, Ruben Schwieger, James Yutzy, and Roy Hoops.

The time finally came for them to pour the floors of the hospital ward. It would be 120 feet by 24 feet—a difficult size without modern equipment, but that did not baffle them. Frank, by this time, had established rapport with his workers and they were just as enthusiastic as he was. He would say, "Fellows, this is going to take us two days to finish. Can we do it?" Back would come one loud united sound, a drawn-out *"Endio Bwana"* [surely]. They knew how well they would be treated because they had worked with him before. So with plenty of food and tea available, they began their work and never stopped until it was finished. They had to work around the clock in order to finish in two days, but they succeeded. Frank kept cheerful and radiated a great deal of contagious enthusiasm. The Africans liked that.

Frank told us that when he returned thirty years later and lovingly rubbed his hands over the walls of the hospital, there wasn't a crack. It was solid!

This was followed by building Mwihila High School, which replacing the teacher training center, including classroom units, teachers' houses, and all the other necessary buildings required to develop an adequate high school program.

**City and Town Churches**

By 1955, the city and town churches needed buildings. Gradually, the wage earners in the reserve had gone to the cities and towns where they could obtain regular work as servants, laborers, and skilled workers. In most instances, their families remained at home to care for the livestock, gardens, home, and children. Sometimes the families or the young people went with them.

Living away from home imposed many hardships on these who loved their families. Most of the Christians found comfort in the fellowship of their church friends and relatives. No matter where they were, they always found a meeting place for Sunday services. Oftentimes, it was in a deserted school classroom that could be rented for a few hours. Usually another group would be waiting impatiently for their portion of time.

The missionaries always tried to visit them on their way to and from the large cities or to the coast to preach and encourage them. They realized the unsatisfactory conditions under which the city and town worshiped. Being so far from home, they needed the fellowship of their friends where they could spend time together rather than go into the sins and vices everywhere around them.

## Kaloleni Church

Under John Ludwig's leadership in the thirties, the Nairobi council set aside a plot of land to be used by the Church of God for a church building. A lack of funds prevented construction of the building. Gradually, as the zoning of the city changed, this piece of land was in great demand, and, since the zoning for African development was in another part of the city, it was advisable to sell the land, which brought a good price. This money was now available to purchase a plot of land in Kaloleni that was offered by the Nairobi city council.

In 1955, Frank LaFont and his workers went to live and work in Nairobi where they built the present Kaloleni church with a seating capacity of more than three hundred. When I attended an Olunyore morning service, the church was packed. Later that morning, a Kiswahili service would be held there. The building was very useful for the much needed services that the Church of God provided.

Since the building of that church, twelve more congregations have sprung up in the Nairobi area. The Mariakani Center, which is the English-speaking church, was built later from funds supplied by Sunday school groups from the States.

## Nakuru Church

Nakuru was an established and active congregation for many years. When A. W. Baker, founder of our Kima Mission, passed away, he left a legacy to be used for the mission. Frank LaFont again superintended the building of a lovely stone church there. It was not as large as the Kaloleni church, but the need was not as great since Nakuru is a smaller city. This church was called the A. W. Baker Memorial Church.

Through the years, Lydia Hansen and I had often stopped at the Nakuru church on our way to Nairobi. For quite a while, both the Nakuru and the Kaloleni church had missionary societies for women. We termed them our "mail-order societies." Since we did not have opportunity to visit them at regular intervals, we sent materials to them by mail that they would sew and sell there and then return the proceeds to the general fund.

A number of years ago, one of the Nakuru women came to me with tears rolling down her cheeks and requested prayer. She had been married for several years but had no children, a great trial to an African woman. We knelt and asked God to give her a child. When we returned years later, a woman came and took me by the hand after the service and said, "I want to show you something. Do come over here to the side of the church." We walked over slowly as she reminded me of the time we had had prayer together many years before.

Before me stood eight children of various sizes. "These are what God gave me," she announced proudly. I greeted each one and heard their names as they each responded with a knowing smile. They must have heard their mother tell that story over many times. Not being sure how to respond to the situation, I wondered if she wanted me to tell God that these were enough!

Though Frank did not go as a builder, he offered to do it until the Missionary Board could find someone.

### Kisii Receives Land for Mission

When A. F. Gray was in Kenya in 1953, the chief in Kisii (Ibeno) requested that a mission be started. Lydia and I had been going down part time for about three years, helping in the churches, schools, and dispensary. A. F. Gray, Frank LaFont, and a number of African leaders went down to Ibeno and stayed with Obed and Miriam Kutera in their little mud hut. Obed was a missionary to Kisii, sent and supported by the Church of God in Bunyore through the African Women's Missionary Society.

The transaction had already been cleared by the chief. That night when the crowd dispersed, the disgruntled son of the man who had donated the land looked up at the grass roof and was heard to say, "Grass roofs burn easily."

No one wanted to go to bed that night; they all sat up until 2:00 A.M. Finally the need for sleep overcame them, and they went to the small room to which they were assigned. Before going to bed, Frank said to A. F., "If this grass roof catches fire tonight, that little hole there for a window is mine."

They measured the plot of ground and this is the place Lydia and I began the mission and lived part time for nearly six years. We often thought about the grass roof and always slept with the car keys within reach of our camp cot, for the hundred miles to Kima would have been a long walk.

The next time Frank returned to Ibeno (Kisii) was to build a safari house for us to live in. We had spent many months living in the house provided for us by Obed and Miriam. Miriam always cleaned it especially for us by varnishing the floor with a fresh coat of cow's dung and moving the family out into the cow stable. She and baby Alfred slept in one of the rooms while we occupied the other one. We could never thank them enough for their excellent hospitality which would make most of us feel ashamed, for I do not have one friend who would go to all that trouble for a guest.

When Frank returned on his errand of mercy—to build a little house for two transient missionaries—he arrived just after one of Kisii's finest rains. The road was muddy—but Kisii had a special characteristic of its own. After a good tropical downpour, the mud becomes chocolate pudding in nature, and it is bottomless. Frank and Margaret managed until they came to the bridge, but it had been washed out. There was nothing else to do except park the pickup along the side of the road and walk the remaining three miles to the mission plot, carrying their luggage, tools, and equipment. Margaret had packed a "chuck box" with food for the stay at Ibeno, but when Frank looked for it, he realized he had left it at home—one-hundred miles away. Fortunately, he liked African food, so for three weeks he ate corn meal mush, chicken, and greens, or whatever was available. But it did not baffle good-natured Frank. They sat in the evenings by the old kerosene lantern, had their devotions, and joked until bedtime.

How thankful we were for that new corrugated metal house. It was home away from home.

**Sisal, Coffee, and Tea Plantation Churches**

Once a year, during their vacation time enroute to Mombasa on the coast, Margaret and Frank planned to visit the different tea, coffee, and sisal estates. Many of our church men and women were employed there, and they spent a night or two with them holding services and baptizing those who wanted to be baptized. The owners were always very happy to have the missionaries come and would provide them with lodging.

On one occasion when they visited a large coffee estate, several people wanted to be baptized. After the Sunday service, Musa Shippira, one of the Kisa elders, took them to a large river for baptism. Several men were in the water with large sticks and poles, and Frank could not understand the reason for this. He asked one of the men about it.

"Oh, that river is full of crocodiles, and we had our clubs ready to chase the crocodiles away."

The next morning when they began their trip south, Frank said to Musa, "I was real proud of you yesterday when you went into the water with those men standing around you with poles. You know why they were there, don't you?"

"No, why?"

"There were crocodiles in the water. They were there to strike them if necessary. I'll bring you again next year to baptize."

"What are you talking about?" Musa questioned. "There is no need to tempt the Lord twice."

As they moved on to another group at a sisal estate near Taveta, they were detained because there were so many elephants on the road. In Kenya, signs are posted, "Elephants have the right of way." No one ever disagrees.

Instead of being met by a European manager, they were met by an Asian named Titus Mattheyo. Frank, curious as always, asked him how he ever received a Christian name, for most Indians he knew were given Indian names such as Patel, Singh, or Jagivan. Then he explained, "Back in the first century, a man by the name of St. Thomas came to South India and he told us the story of a man called Jesus Christ. There are still many of the Christians who date their linear history back to the time when St. Thomas came to South India."

From there they went on to Mombasa. Living at a mile-high altitude at Kima, it is necessary for the foreign missionaries to go to sea level for a vacation about once a year. They soon contacted the church there and had services with them.

## Uganda

Margaret and Frank were sent to Uganda by the African assembly after their return from one of their furloughs. A Church of God congregation of Luyia-speaking Africans were living there without a pastor. The sum of twenty-five thousand dollars had been raised while they were on furlough to build a church in Uganda, but due to the strained political situations, they were unable to buy land at that time. However, they organized Sunday schools in three different housing areas. A new congregation was started on one of the large agricultural schemes north of Kampala. During the time the LaFonts were there, seventeen persons were baptized. A young pastor named Rufus Akhonya came from Kenya to help them as pastor of the two churches they were able to start. Another church was started near Tororo. The churches were attended by the Bunyore people who lived and worked there. Not until later were they able to reach the Buganda people.

Frank relates a story about a Buganda man who came inquiring:

*He asked us about an ad we'd put in the paper advertising the meetings of the Church of God. He said there is only one church in the Bible, so he wanted us to explain what we believed. Our beliefs were identical, so we went with him about twenty miles toward the Congo border west of Kampala and helped him get a church started. We encouraged the group by paying for the church's metal roof.*

*After seventeen months, everything seemed to be going well as far as the church was concerned, but political unrest, was causing a great deal of confusion. Byrum Makokha, executive secretary of the Church of God Assembly in Kenya, wrote, warning us to leave. We quietly shipped our things to Mombasa and headed for the border. The Tororo folks didn't think we would get through, but we were able to get our car across the border. The Africans from Kenya left, too. We hear now that some of the people are still worshiping in the church at Kigumu and Soroti. We are thrilled about it. The Hoffmans have gone to work there now. They still have Rufus Akhonya working with them.*

Rufus was one of the men who went down to work with the Masai. He and Willie Okaya started a work near the Uganda border during the time they were in the Kima Theological College. They are two fine pioneer pastors.

When Margaret and Frank were forced to leave Uganda, they were invited to come to Mombasa to build a church there.

## Mombasa Church

The LaFonts not only built the church in Mombasa, but stayed and helped that church for two and a half years. They started vacation schools and pastored, going frequently to Chimgabwe, a small congregation outside Mombasa, to preach. The Chimgabwe meetings were held under the coconut trees. One Sunday when rain disrupted the service, Frank said to the congregation, "Why don't you folks get a piece of land and I'll build you a church." A few months later, the people came to the house as a delegation and said, "Bwana, we have something we want to show you." So he went with them to Chimgabwe. They said, "See the plot of land over there? That's ours."

"Where did you get it?" Frank inquired, surprised.

"We've been saving money for some time, and we bought it. Now we are ready for you to build a church."

Then Frank related that for a long time he had been saving

money that people had been sending to them for churches. So they began the little 24-by-40-foot church with the funds that had accumulated, but they ran out of cash before the building was finished. When Herschell Rice was visiting and Frank was showing him around, Frank told Herschell that they had not finished the chapel because they had run out of money.

"How much will it take?" he asked.

"I'll need a thousand dollars," Frank replied. Herschell did not say anything, but after returning home, he wrote us this letter:

"I came home and preached Sunday morning. That night, when standing at the door, one of our parishioners said, 'Pastor, guess what! I got a thousand dollars back from my income tax and don't know what to do with it.'

"Well, I told him to give it to me and I'd send it to Frank LaFont to finish his church. So I'm sending you a check for one thousand dollars."

Frank said, "We were able to finish the chapel and spent two and a half years there encouraging the people."

### Kiligoris, Masai

Frank and Margaret came back to retire in Walla Walla, Washington, at the end of their mission service, and, after a few years, they went back to Kenya to help the Masai. A group of seventeen men from Washington and California went to build the building at Kiligoris. Frank relates,

*We went under Vacation Samaritans to Kisii and stayed at the mission in Ibeno, where Lima Lehmer [Williams] and Lydia Hansen [McDonald] lived for so long. We went every day to Kiligoris, but we did not have all the materials we needed, so we were able to put up a metal building for them with three rooms and lay the foundations for the big church. We put up a part of the walls and filled in the floor with soil, for it was very high. We had to leave and did not get to finish it. When my tour group was in Kenya, we passed Kiligoris on our way to Kisii. They had finished the building. They have a nice center there now for the Masai people. We were proud to have had a hand in it there.*

# Chapter 35

# Mwihila Develops

After Jewell had been in Mwihila for about nine months, Irene Engst, a Canadian, came in 1947 to assist with the work. The Kisa people did not want Irene to stop at Kima, for they were afraid if she stopped there, they would never get her. So they pleaded with Jewell to bring her home by another road. Jewell complied and bypassed Kima. A heavy rainstorm had filled the gutters with hail. In spite of the storm and cold weather that detained them for more than two hours, the people waited along the road to welcome their first missionary who had come to them without being tainted by Kima. She was theirs!

In order to show Irene how much they wanted her, they presented her with a sheep. A great honor indeed!

Jewell was relieved to have a co-worker. Now she would be released from treating the sick, a task that greatly interfered with her classroom work. Irene had taken missionary medical training for about a year and was able to treat the ordinary cases. The extraordinary ones had to be taken to the goverment hospital at Kakamega. Since Irene had not yet learned to drive, she would help Jewell in the classroom while Jewell would take the patients to the hospital. They soon began to work together as a team.

A few years before, one of the nurses who had been trained

at the maternity hospital had come to help Jewell with the sick patients. When Irene came, Mabel continued. But there was still no building in which to work. One looks at the beautiful Mwihila Hospital and may think it has always been there. Not so; Irene began it. She was a Canadian and knew how to cope with a rugged life. Her father was a sheep farmer in British Columbia, and Irene had learned at an early age how to work in a pioneer country. So she did as she always had been used to doing, making the best of an impossible situation to make it possible. She gathered her medications and bandages up in a basket, chose a place along the road, and began treatments under a tree. One of the men made a table for her, a few poles were set up for seats, and the the crowd began to come.

At first she treated the general run of cases found in most African dispensaries. Gradually, the maternity cases began to come for help.

This presented another problem, for they did not have accommodations for such cases. Time was valuable; the trip of forty miles to Kakamega and back was not always possible for Jewell, and Irene did not drive. A solution was found by constructing a mud and wattle hut. The African women carried the grass for the roof and mudded the walls under the supervision of Musa Shippira, one of our strong African elders. Irene remained in her under-tree dispensary until it was finished. Many and varied were her experiences as she tended the sick. Sometimes the cases were most urgent and immediate care was necessary. One of her patients came with a snake bite, but the serum was too late to save her. Esther Joshua, one of Irene's faithful women workers, was bitten by a black mamba snake while gathering firewood. Her son was near and was able to tie a tourniquet on her upper arm before putting her on his bicycle and rushing her to the dispensary. Esther did recover, though she regained her strength slowly. How thankful Irene was that Esther's life was spared, for in later years she became one of her strongest helpers in the womens society work.

One day while Irene was treating patients under the tree, the crowd suddenly began to run. As she looked up she saw a cobra hanging in the tree above her, spitting down at the patients. Fortunately it did not hit anyone.

The tree dispensary continued for about a year and a half before the treatment room was finished. That did not discourage the patients. A maternity case came before the beds arrived, but she was delivered on the floor. When the building was completed, other needs became evident. The grass roof provided shelter, but they needed water to carry on their work.

The next project involved a galvanized metal roof with a rain tank. Soon the mud walls were replaced with metal ones lined with plaster board. The improved building was better able to be kept in a sanitary condition as the delivery room and treatment center.

As in all temporary buildings, this one, too, had its drawbacks. Vera Martin laughed when she told how all of the small linens were disappearing—baby shirts, washcloths, and such. Not knowing where they were going, she challenged the employees about them. Years later when the building was torn down, after the new hospital had been built, she found all of her lost articles between the walls where they had been carried by the pack rats that had been so plentiful in the dispensary.

The ill health and death of Jewell Hall's father in 1949 took her away on furlough.

In 1950, David and Elsie Gaulke, on their way home from China, came to look over the possibility of building a hospital at Mwihila. As David looked across the road, he said, "I think that is where the hospital should be built."

Even though it was not on mission property, Elder Musa Shippira began working, and by the time the Gaulkes returned in 1953, the land had been acquired for the building.

Since Irene was left alone, the mission asked Mabel Baker if she would be willing to fill in while Jewell was on furlough. Mabel, our senior missionary, had never been known to hesitate to serve wherever needed, and she graciously went to live at Mwihila. Teacher training was not new to Mabel, for she had trained most of the teachers who were now working in our elementary schools. So with Irene and Timothy Litondo, she took Jewell's place in an effort to take the present class through to graduation.

With Jewell gone, no one was there who could drive, so all travel for the observations of the teachers had to be done by foot. The schools where the students were doing their practicum in teaching were not always near the mission, but this presented no great problem for our seasoned pioneer missionary, just three years away from retirement. For years she had disciplined herself to walk to many of the faraway villages in Bunyore to inspect schools, teach Sunday school classes, preach, or whatever was needed.

So with a thermos of tea, her old felt hat, a bag with her teaching materials, comfortable shoes, and an umbrella, she set out with Irene. Walking seemed to invigorate her. Irene and Jewell, too, had been conditioned for the long walks with their students before the days when the teacher training center was able to afford a truck to take groups to their schools.

Through the kindness of the Kima missionaries, they were able to get their groceries delivered to them. Irene mentions one occasion when she and Mabel needed to go to Kisumu for business. The Yala train station was five miles from the mission, and so they walked there, took the train, spent the day in Kisumu, and walked back again from the station in the evening. One wonders how many miles they walked about Kisumu in addition to the ten miles to and from the station.

Irene was delighted to have the privilege of knowing and working with Mabel Baker. She was always occupied in translation work and, being British, was somewhat reserved. Mabel was a sage and could give excellent help to young missionaries in language, native mores, and taboos. How she helped me in the very early days and through the years that followed!

Frank LaFont oversaw the fixing of the mission house and made it much more livable. The LaFonts were fine companions who eased the loneliness for Irene with their visits.

After Jewell's return from furlough, Irene was at last free to begin missionary societies in the villages with the women. Both women spent their Sundays in the villages, helping to strengthen the churches.

The Kisa women launched their program by giving Irene a sheep. They were delighted to have a womens organization in their churches. Not only was she able to teach them Bible, but she also gave them an outreach in missions through their sewing groups. By this time, Irene had learned to drive and was now more independent.

Things began to move quickly now at Mwihila. Hazel McDilda arrived in 1951 and relieved Irene from the dispensary work, and so Irene was able to increase her womens work, which continued to grow and prosper. They were able to share in some of the outreach programs that the womens groups of the three mission stations now sponsored. The groups helped build the first dispensary in Kisii at the Ibeno station one hundred miles away. Their proceeds from sewing helped keep the babies warm at night and reduced the pneumonia cases considerably, as well as provided money for the advancement of the churches.

Chapter 36

# The Schwiegers
# Go to Ingotse

In 1947, Ruben and Nora Schwieger with their three children answered God's call to missionary service in Kenya Colony. Ruben had been in Kima only a few days when his predecessor, Herman Smith, handed him the huge set of keys and turned the Kima Boys School over to him.

Ruben said, "Although I had taught school and had been superintendent of small schools and principal of larger ones, I found the junior secondary school at Kima under the British educational system vastly different from what I had been used to. I found that the boys were not really boys at all, but grown men, all over twenty years of age. In school they slept on the floor, ate cornmeal mush, and had crude implements to work with. There were no discipline problems, for if one was expelled, others were waiting to take his place."

He laughed, as did the rest of us, at a few of the mistakes he made as a new missionary. The first Sunday there, he was asked to preach at the Kima church. He chose as his text Galatians 6:11. He used a modern translation that read, "Don't kid yourself, God is not mocked." His interpreter winked, blinked, stuttered, and finally said, "Don't get yourself with child." American idioms are not understood very well by Africans.

Another time when he went with Herman Smith to a village, he saw two old men making something from grass. He had already learned two words, and, trying to be friendly, he proceeded to use both of them. The first was the greeting, *Milembe,* or peace. The second was *Nobulahi,* meaning "it is good."

Herman Smith looked at him with one of his big grins and said, "Ruben, do you know what those old men were making?"

"No, I just wanted to be friendly and encourage them in whatever they were doing."

"Those were beer strainers they were making to go to a beer drink."

The Schwiegers lived for six months at Kima. Ruben taught in the boys school and Nora taught domestic science in the girls school. When the school year had finished, they moved to Ingotse.

The following is an account of their arrival, given by Ruben:

*On the 24th day of December 1947, when we moved to Ingotse, the sight that met our eyes we shall never forget. The yard was literally full of people! Halt, lame, sick, legs that were covered with ulcers, some very large, children with their toes full of chigger fleas, and some with burning fever from malaria.*

*I never saw such a frustrated look on my wife's face before. This group of lost suffering humanity was looking straight to her for help. Naturally, we had planned to unload our things from the truck and get settled down and prepare for what we thought would be our missionary work. These plans we had to lay aside now and see what we could do for these expectant people.*

*It dawned upon us that there had been no missionaries stationed at Ingotse for a long time—no kind hands to treat the sick, no loving heart to share a concern for the sorrowing, no outstretched hand to help in time of trouble, and no sharing of food in time of famine. This is what showed so clearly on those upturned faces. My wife had had no training as a nurse. Her major in college was home economics, and she did have a course in first aid, but what was needed here was a registered nurse and a doctor. Neither one was available.*

*Instead of unloading the furniture, we pulled an old sheet from one of our boxes, tore it into strips to use for bandages, washed the sores with soap and water, and bandaged them up. We dug chigger fleas from the children's toes, painted the holes*

*where the egg bag had been with iodine, gave quinine and
aspirin to the ones who had fever, had prayer for all of them,
and sent them home. Not many words were spoken, for we did
not know their language, but a smile, a clean bandage, and a
prayer needed no words. This was the beginning of a work that
was to take most of my wife's time for the next five years—that
of caring for the sick around the Ingotse mission. Sometimes
as many as a hundred cases would be treated in a day.*

For two years Nora took care of the sick people under a
large rubber tree in front of the house. Then the women from
Oklahoma made some money available to the Missionary
Board and a dispensary building was built so that she had a
place to care for the sick. She needed a helper and finally
found Marita, a girl who knew English and was able to help
her with the patients. Nora's little girls worked with her and in
no time at all WillaRae had picked up quite a few words from
the African children. It did not take Nora long either to learn
the language, and she became quite fluent with it before
leaving Kenya.

Ingotse had not been inhabited for a long time; the land was
overgrown. There was a small three-room school building
that had been used for classrooms. Another old building had
been used by Mrs. William Bailey for a lying-in ward for the
sick. This could be cleaned and used for a dormitory.

The government had given a small grant of 1,000 pounds,
less than three thousand dollars, to build a classroom block
and teachers' houses. So beginning with the four oxen owned
by the mission, which were now in the care of a neighbor, and
a walking plow and *jembes* [hoes], Ruben and his 105 helpers
cleared the land. Soon corn, sweet potatoes, and cabbages
were sprouting forth in place of bush. The educational officer
arrived three months later and said, "I have never seen a
wilderness turned into a Garden of Eden in such a short time."

This was only the beginning. Much water was needed for
105 boys and the two dug wells had long before gone dry. The
effort to secure water included a number of trial and error
methods, mostly failures. They began by digging a well only to
find that it had caved in before morning. The dry season had
begun, hence, no rain could be expected during the months of
December, January, and February. This meant hauling water
for about three quarters of a mile. So they tied a forty-gallon
drum on a sled made from the fork of a tree and used the oxen
to pull the sled. Carrying all the water needed for the school
was an endless task.

Ruben could not give up. The next effort to dig a well was to get an old galvanized tank with the bottom removed and slip it down as they dug. This prevented the cave-ins. At thirty-five feet they found water. A brick layer was employed to reinforce the walls of the well. In a short time, this well went dry. Ruben had heard of a ram, but had no experience with one. He finally went to Eldoret and bought one. They warned him that he would have to have the water dropping down into it before it would function. Ingotse has a level terrain. He persevered and attempted several ways to get the water. He made several dams before it worked properly. All methods worked for a short time and then he had to begin over again.

Ruben was concerned about his lack of patience but he kept trying. In the following story, he mentions impatience as being expensive:

*I got tired of hauling water for use in our kitchen, and so I decided to buy a thousand-gallon galvanized tank and set it up on a tower near our kitchen so that the rains could fill it from the roof and the water from the tank could run by gravity into our kitchen. The roof of our house wasn't very high, and so I could only build the rock tower about six feet high. I became impatient for the cement to dry properly and a rain was coming up, so I decided to let the water run into the tank.*

*We had a tropical downpour that afternoon and the tank was soon filled to overflowing. About the middle of the night, we were awakened by a tremendous crash that shook the whole house. The foundation had given away under the tank and a thousand gallons of water made the tank look like a tin can we used for playing hockey at school. Impatience can be expensive. This time it cost me the price of a new tank, several bags of cement, and a week's work.*

*I had to seek the Lord earnestly because of this fault of impatience and ask him to help me overcome this weakness. Thank God, there came a time when I gained complete victory over it and was able to keep calm under all circumstances.*

The humility of this godly servant can only be appreciated by the love and patience he showed those with whom he worked.

### School Problems for the Children

Ruben Don was in his second year at Rift Valley Academy, but when Kathleen became ready for school, there was no room there for her, so it was necessary to find another school for her first year. They found that the Kaimosi Friends Mission, about thirty miles away, could take her, and so they enrolled her there. She stayed in the home of one of the missionaries and returned home every two weeks. This was both time consuming and inconvenient.

The next year there was a vacancy at Rift Valley Academy and Kathleen went with Ruben Don to school. During that year the principal wrote that Ruben Don had contracted rheumatic fever and asked his parents to take him home for three months' bed rest.

Ruben went to get him and he expresses the deep emotional moments which overpowered him:

*I think the most heart-rending moment I have ever had in all my life was when I loaded Ruben Don into the car at Kijabe and drove away leaving Kathleen, only seven years old, standing there in the yard alone, two hundred and fifty miles from home.*

*I had to turn my face so that she could not see the tears that began to flow down my cheeks. I noticed that the brave little thing held up much better than I did. I was ashamed.*

*In three months Ruben Don was well again. He had missed his friends and one day, when he had received a letter, I heard him ask God for strength. Ruben Don had become a Christian at our family altar. He had already learned to whom to turn in times of trial and loneliness.*

*The next year we had all the indications of a happy beginning. All three had been accepted at Kijabe. They had had a good time at home and were all making plans to return to school together when a polio epidemic struck. Russell Renz, who had come with his wife, Velma, to take my place while we went on furlough, was the first to be stricken. The disease paralyzed both his legs, and in 1952 he and Velma had to be flown home.*

WillaRae was next to come down with the dreaded disease, but when the children took their physicals later, they suffered no permanent effects from either the rheumatic fever or the polio.

The Schwiegers went on furlough in 1952 and returned again in 1953.

A number of changes affected the missions. The schools were changed from junior secondary schools to intermediate schools. These schools were taken over by the government. Government grants were cut in half and boarding grants were decreased, and eventually they would be withdrawn. An African headmaster replaced the European principal with African teachers in charge. The medical department had passed a new ruling that only trained people would be permitted to treat the sick.

The Mau Mau uprising broke out, and this again changed the children's educational plans. Since the greater part of the Mau Mau activity was in the Kikuyu area where the Rift Valley Academy was located, the administrators would not give the smaller children permission to return to school. Ruben Don could attend Kijabe, but the school could not be responsible for the very young children. Another school had to be found for Kathleen and WillaRae. Finally they were able to go to the Mara Hills Mennonite Mission in Tanganyika [presently Tanzania]. The school was across Lake Victoria and the little girls were put on the lake steamer at Kisumu for an overnight trip and met the next morning by the missionaries there.

Again we feel with the parents, making this great sacrifice. Ruben states, "It was hard to send two little girls alone over Lake Victoria on the steamer at night. The only thing we could do was to commit them into the hands of the Lord."

A number of years later, the Missionary Board started an elementary school at Mwihila for the mission children with missionary Vivian Phelps as their teacher. This was the time when Mau Mau insurrection was taking place, and oaths were being taken to kill a white person. Much of this occurred in the mountain region near the Rift Valley Academy. Carl Kardatzke was there the night of the greatest raid by the Mau Mau. The police asked all of the older boys to stand guard up in the hills just above the mission. Carl's son, Howdie, took his place as a guard with the other boys, while his father sat with a long machete in his hands. Persons knowing Carl could not imagine him on anything but a peace mission, but this was for the protection of the students. That night, many of the people were slaughtered in the hills directly above Kijabe, but they did not oppress the mission. It was a night of atrocities and a time when Christians went through great persecutions. It was a time of cleansing for the Kikuyu church.

With all the changes that took place, both Ruben and Nora felt burdened for the people of the villages. The need in the churches was great. Though Ruben and Nora had formerly been occupied with the school and the dispensary, now they were free to do the spiritual work of God. This seemed to be the answer to their prayers.

They first began at home, and Ruben expressed the need as he preached at Ingotse:

*The first Sunday I preached in church at Ingotse, I could not even see to read the text. The church building was made of low rock and mud walls, with a huge overhanging grass roof, one door, and a few small windows. On this first Sunday I said to myself that with the help of the Lord, I would build a new church building here!*

One night around the dinner table, Ruben and Nora shared a number of their frustrating experiences. As I listened I suddenly recalled Jim Murray sitting at the same place they were sitting many years before, telling of the same hopes that Ruben and Nora had for a church at Ingotse. We investigated using a memorial gift from Jim's late wife, Ruth, for construction of the much-needed building. Fortunately, the money was still available and it was sent for the church building. There was not enough money to build the type of church they needed, but they began on faith. Much of the work was donated labor. When the Africans heard of the money gift, they said, "We have never heard of people giving a gift after they died. They loved us so much."

The text of Ruben's sermon at the dedication of Murray Memorial Chapel was John 4:38: "I sent you to reap whereon ye bestowed no labor; other men have labored and ye are entered into their labors." This text had a humbling effect on us. For that is what our mission work has been in Kenya— reaping from the labor of those who have gone on before. "Paul planted, Apollos watered, but God gave the increase."

The people of Ingotse were widely scattered. Missionary effort had been in the area for years but, because of lack of continuity of staff, it had not had the nurture required for steady growth. The Murrays tried to supply that need and went to the people in their villages, and Ruth had given her life in their effort to do this. God still had his hand on Ingotse and brought Ruben and Nora to do the task the Murrays were unable to complete. He chose the right people. Often they mentioned how they loved Ingotse, which reminded them of the Panhandle in Oklahoma.

Many changes had to be made, and they sought ways to improve what was there and to replace what needed replacement. The old mission house where they first lived had six large bedrooms on the second floor and had been built by Homer Bailey for a large family. Mud-covered walls had become inhabited by swarms of bees and termites. The missionaries needed a new home. Ruben soon erected a new residence where his family could live comfortably. The old dilapidated school buildings were pulled down and replaced by the new school rooms and teacher houses supplied by the government.

During the first five years, everything was placed in order so that normal living was possible. The school was separated and designated as government property and placed at one end of the mission. The mission was along the public road where it was available to the people.

The Calvin Bralliers came to Ingotse while the Schwiegers were on furlough and took charge of the boys school in 1952-53. After the Bralliers left, the boys school ultimately became a secondary school. Bill and Kathy Delisle came with Clyde and Rowena Harting to teach in the new high school. Later Robert and Janet Edwards and several others joined the teaching staff.

In 1952, Jane Ryan came to Ingotse as the first registered nurse. She lived in the old mission house until a suitable one could be built for her.

With all these physical needs cared for, Ruben and Nora were free to do the thing they had always hoped to do—go to the people with the word of God.

None of the thirteen struggling congregations in the district had a permanent church building. They began with a regular schedule. The Murrays had attempted this type of work when Ruth became ill with the typhoid fever that proved fatal. However, the Schwiegers were better prepared for safari living, for they had better transportation in their Volkswagen van. Now that they no longer had the responsibility of the school and the dispensary, they were able to give most of their time for evangelization in the churches and teaching the pastors.

They planned to spend Tuesday, Wednesday, and Thursday of each week visiting two villages every day. Nora conducted classed for the women, teaching them Bible and sewing. The women needed to find their place in the church program. During that time Ruben would visit the homes with the pastor until 11 A.M. and then teach a Bible class to all who would come for the service. From 1 P.M. to 4 P.M. they followed the same procedure in another village. It was during these visits that they became very close to the leaders and learned about their problems.

As they studied their needs, they identified them as evangelization, organization, and finance, and they set a goal to try to reach them. They also sensed a great need for teaching and guidance. Most of the pastors had only a hymnal and a Luyia Testament from which to preach. They had had few opportunities for education. The elders of the district had had more opportunities to attend conventions and, for the most part, were better educated.

The churches were all of mud and wattle with grass roofs. The people had little money, but they brought grain offerings that were used for the poor and needy, and perhaps some went to the pastor.

The women needed teaching, too. Nora began sewing classes with them. She then set aside a part of the time for Bible teaching and she worked with the Sunday school teachers by providing adequate lesson materials for them. From their sewing they were able to earn some money to provide equipment for the church.

Ruben began his task with the pastors. Many of the churches were without any equipment. When they met, they carried the pastor's table into the church for use as a pulpit. The people sat on the floor unless they brought their own chairs to sit on. So he began a series of lectures on finance. He preached tithing until they said to each other when they saw him coming, "Here comes Bwana Tithe." He taught them how to keep books and give reports to the people. It finally caught on, and when the people realized where their money was going, they felt encouraged to give more. The church soon became an important place in their lives.

Then the Schwiegers began to challenge them by offering to buy the board windows and doors when they would complete a permanent or semipermanent church building. For fifteen years, they spent their time working with the people of the villages, teaching, counseling, encouraging, and loving them into the kingdom of God. I asked Ruben and Nora to share some of the high points of their twenty years of missionary service and he sent me his book, *Paths for God.* He has summed up his work as follows:

*Every boy who went through the boys school during the five years I was principal there became a Christian before he left the school. We completed several buildings: a classroom block to accommodate 140 boys, five teacher's houses, three dormitories, a carpenter shop, a tailor shop and a library; a dispensary building where the sick could more easily be treated; the* **Murray Memorial Chapel,** *a home for the missionary, and a nurse's residence.*

*During the fifteen years after the school was turned over to the Africans, Nora and I spent the time with the churches. They grew in number from 11 to 36, each with a pastor, and of the 36 congregations, half of them had either semipermanent or permanent buildings. Every congregation had adopted a tithing system for its support. Each pastor received some instruction in Bible study, sermon preparation, and church business training. Another great joy was assisting in baptizing hundreds of believers.*

Before retirement, Ruben and his interpreters spent every day in the villages. They would conduct meetings with the people, using their van for sleeping and eating.

With all these activities, they never neglected their family. They enjoyed recreational trips with the children during vacations. At one time, they took the family to visit Victoria Falls in northern Rhodesia and took frequent hunting and fishing trips with the children. They were a very devoted family.

We have mentioned Ruben's expertise in so many different areas, but Nora excelled in everything she did, too. She was an expert cook, seamstress, and homemaker. She was a very creative person and quite knowledgeable. Having spent time in Hawaii as a teacher, she had a marvelous ability to give all the botanical names of the tropical plants. Not only was she a wonderful mother and an efficient nurse, but above all, she was a dependable Christian who loved the work of God.

After Jane Ryan left on furlough, Vera Martin moved to Ingotse as the nurse.

## Chapter 37

# Lydia Hansen Arrives

In 1949 Lydia Hansen arrived in Kenya with Jewell Hall. At about the same time, David and Elsie Gaulke arrived on their way to the United States from China. Because of the communist revolution, they had left western China hurriedly by way of Burma, taking with them the few articles they were able to carry. They stopped in Kenya to see what the possibilities were to begin a hospital there.

During their stay, Herman Smith and his son, Paul, took Dave Gaulke on a hunting trip several hundred miles from the mission. Paul developed appendicitis, and since it was impossible to drive him over the rough terrain, they were at a loss to know what to do. Paul became worse and the appendix ruptured. Dr. Gaulke, a surgeon, had no instruments with him and, seeing Paul's grave condition, knew he must have immediate help if Paul were to recover.

At that time, the MGM studios were filming *Solomon's Mines* nearby. An appeal was sent to MGM for air transport. A landing strip was prepared where they were marooned. MGM kindly flew Paul back to the Kisumu hospital. By this time he was in a very serious condition with peritonitis. Nurses were summoned from nearby missions and remained with him around the clock. Dr. Gaulke wanted to operate, but since he did not have a Kenyan license, the British doctors refused.

Finally the doctors operated on Paul, but he did not gain consciousness for several days and took weeks to recover fully.

Lydia served as Paul's nurse at Kisumu Hospital, her first nursing experience in an African-English hospital. Everyone agreed that Paul's recovery was only in answer to prayer.

Lydia was assigned to the Kima Hospital. She moved in with me, and we spent twelve happy years together. Recently she wrote about her impressions of the early days:

*I worked in the hospital and knew so little about tropical diseases. The hospital had several side rooms with one on the outside. It had a grass roof and* esingo *floors. I remember during the rainy season seeing the flying ants coming out of the walls and the African patients eating them as they flew out. Rita, one of our nurses, had gathered a half-gallon jar full that she was taking home to her children to eat. That was a delicacy the children loved.*

*Nursing was certainly on a different level here than at home. One patient was a woman who had been bitten twice by a snake while resting in her bed. I gave her snake serum but it was too late.*

*Burn cases were horrible. Often we had to bandage patients all over their bodies. We used many bandages on these cases. They often became septic if they have been treated first by the Africans. I have seen them put ink, eggs, rabbit fur, grease, and cow's dung on the wounds of one child. That child died of tetanus.*

*In one burn case a woman came into the hospital in labor. Her dress had caught fire and 90 percent of her body had been burned. She delivered in that condition, with second- and third-degree burns. There wasn't a spot on her body where I could touch her during delivery. Her baby was born and she began to recover, but in spite of our care, she died, and the baby died a short time later.*

*Since many cases resulted from drunken brawls, this provided a good time to preach to them. I had a funny case at Kima. It was a young boy with a cut just under his right eye. I had put sterile towels around his eyes and was ready to put in an injection of Novocaine when he pulled away his head. My nurse, Flora, flew at him and said in a stern voice, "What's the matter with you? Haven't you been circumcised?" After a boy has been circumcised, he is supposed to be able to be brave and endure pain without flinching, and this young, single nurse was from his own clan. No girl would ever marry a coward. I think I could have sewn him up without an anesthetic after that—he was so ashamed.*

*Another time I was suturing a woman while I was sick with malaria. It was not a sight anyone would want to tackle when well. But while I was nauseated and sick, it was that much harder. I had to sit down, put my head between my knees, trying to get my bearings, and then return to suture again. I had to do that several times before I finished the job. She must have had a hundred or so stitches. I had to suture inside and then outside again.*

*Once a drunken man came in, all cut up over his face, and all the time I was suturing him, I gave him an evangelistic message.*

*One man came into the Mwihila hospital with cuts all over both legs, arms, back, and abdomen. Dr. David Livingston and I packed him with gauze saturated with antiseptic for a few days. Then Dr. Livingston took one side of him, stitching each wound, I took the other, and we turned him on his tummy to do his back. He walked out of the hospital in about a week without an infection anywhere.*

*I pulled several teeth and decided it wasn't for me. Fortunately, we had Leah, our senior nurse, who was an excellent tooth puller. It hurt me as much as the patient. I just couldn't do it.*

*Leah was the daughter of Atetwi, the first Christian girl to be baptized by the Richardsons back in the earliest days of the mission. Atetwi's Christian name became Mariamu. Leah was just as faithful and steady as her mother and made a similar contribution to the mission. Our three trained nurses were Leah, Sara Kalebu, and Rita Paulo—three wonderful nurses.*

At one time we seemed to have an epidemic of tetanus patients coming into the hospital, mostly among newborn infants. Apparently some animals had become infected with tetanus and, since cow's dung was used on the floors at that time, the babies became infected too. They all seemed to come from the same district. Babies were brought in with spasms, their backs arched like a bow, and with tight jaws. Lydia experimented with the tetanus serum, using the serum and reducing it to one-eighth of the adult dose, and feeding lactogen through a tube into the baby's stomach every three hours for about a week or so. They showed improvement and the next two cases recovered, but the third one died as did the mother who had tetanus when the baby was born.

Lydia wrote these cases up for the medical society. Many of the doctors had not come in contact with similar cases, so it was a new discovery for the treatment of tetanus neotorium.

The cases increased. Each day brought different and more challenging ones. Lydia's Canadian-German pioneer background never knew defeat. She usually handled them cheerfully and with a smile. A few things upset her—like injustices to people.

As Africans became trained as dressers or orderlies, sometimes the drop-outs used their knowledge for profit in deceptive forms of treatment for the sick in the villages. The hypodermic needle that had become a magic cure for any ailment, now became a force of ill repute when used by one of these unscrupulous "doctors." Milk was substituted for penicillin, lemon juice for quinine, and many other substitutions were made through the hypo needle. Wounds as large as walnuts developed from unclean needles. These problems were common, not only at Kima where there was no doctor available, but at Mwihila and every other dispensary.

When Lowry Quinn visited Kima in 1948, he dedicated the new maternity unit at Kima built from funds contributed by churches in the United States. After waiting for nearly twenty-five years, the Africans began to put pressure on the mission for their new general hospital. Years before, they had carried the rocks for its foundations and they were still using the old ant-eaten hospital Twyla Ludwig began. Buildings were being built at the girls school, but not for the hospital.

Once Daudi Otieno came to me and said, in no gentle voice, "Miss Lehmer, why aren't you a Deborah? We must have this hospital." Little did he know how many appeals I had made through letters, pamphlets, and hundreds of vocal appeals while on furlough.

I do not know when the money finally came for it from the United States, but Lydia Hansen and Wick Donohew drew up the plans for the hospital at Kima. In 1951 it was dedicated. Now our nurses were able to work in modern surroundings! Their uniforms remained white longer!

## Chapter 38

# Calvin Brallier Becomes Educational Secretary

**W**hen Calvin and Martha Brallier came to Kima in December 1950, we were so happy to see such a fine young couple just out of college. Martha looked so young and pretty with nice new clothes. Ours were now at the point at which they needed to be replaced, while she looked as fresh as if she had just come out of a dress shop.

They began their work at Kima. The LaFonts had gone on furlough and few of us remained on the mission. The Donohews were still there and Wick Donohew took a great interest in Calvin. They soon developed a close relationship. Calvin continues to remember the wise counseling he received through Wick Donohew as he observed him working with the Africans and the missionaries. What a privilege to have such wise guidance when one begins a first term on the mission.

Cal became the educational secretary of the Church of God mission schools. About fifty schools were in operation when he came. He oversaw their work, hired and paid their teachers, inspected their schools, planned their buildings, and represented the school to the Kenya government.

Since Russell Renz's illness had forced him and Velma to return to the United States, Calvin Brallier volunteered to cover the work from Ingotse as well as from Kima so that the Ruben Schwiegers could proceed with their furlough plans.

As Calvin became more familiar with his work, he was advanced by the government to the position of the provincial educational officer of all the mission schools and was given more help with his work. He now had the responsibility of more than one-thousand schools from five different missions in Nyanza Province.

The educational work of the mission was extensive, and for the most part was supported by government grants to erect and maintain buildings, house teachers, pay teachers' salaries, and provide necessary supplies. All of this was done by the government, while at the same time the mission managed the school operations—employed teachers, gave guidance in religious instruction, supplied pastoral care for the students in the school, utilizing an educational committee appointed by the mission. Even salaries for missionary teachers were paid by the government, the plan being that the government paid into the mission treasury and the missionary teachers were paid by the Missionary Board just as all other missionaries were.

Therefore, when we speak of the mission schools, we include the assistance that comes from the government in Kenya, as well as the large corps of primary, intermediate, teacher training, and Bible school teachers who are Africans. Most of them have come up through the mission schools to assume the posts they now hold.

Calvin ministered to the schools of the Church of God, Friends, African Inland Mission, World Gospel Mission, Church Missionary Society, and Pentecostal Missions in the Nyanza province. Four supervisors, one clerk, and a secretary worked with him. He traveled twenty-five thousand miles annually to visit these schools. Through this very important work, he developed an exceedingly strong youth group led by the teachers.

**Youth Fellowship**

Calvin reports:

*African custom has never allowed the mingling of African young people in fellowship as it is known in the churches in America. Therefore, the organization of a youth fellowship in 1952 was a distinct advancement for the Church of God in*

146

*East Africa. Calvin Brallier was chosen as the counselor, a post he filled for eight years. The fellowship has made great strides and gained great numbers. A yearly convention is held in November and it has grown in attendance every year. It has not been easy to promote youth work in the churches, but the fact that most of the leaders were also teachers in the mission schools has helped a great deal in overcoming the old customs in force for centuries. Such customs cannot be broken in a few years; many of them have value, and the church would suggest changes only if they would be better for the people.*

*It took time to reach the younger youth, but gradually, by working with the teachers, it became very successful and both sexes were able to work together. Rallies, conventions, and youth-centered activities became a part of their strong Christian program. Missionaries James Yutzy, Carl Kardatzke, and a number of others participated from time to time to make it a success.*

*A representative from the Council of Churches of Geneva, Switzerland, came to Kenya to observe the youth groups. At the suggestion of the leaders in Nairobi, he was directed to Calvin Brallier. He was so satisfied with what he saw that he wrote it up in* Glover's World Mission Textbook.

## Shitoli Mission

One day when Calvin went into the government office in Kakamega, the commissioner told him that a new missionary family, the Roy Hoopses, were living at the old gold mine. Did he know them?

The next Sunday, coming home from a village church service, they passed the home of Roy and Magaline Hoops, and Calvin said, "Martie, let's stop to visit the Hoopses."

This was one of the outposts that the Ludwigs' independent mission had begun in the heart of the Church of God territory. They received them cordially but somewhat distantly. Calvin disarmed them by saying, "You and Magaline have come to serve the Lord. You have no animosity against the Church of God and we have no feelings against you, but you must remember that the Africans go back in history before we came, and they have memories. Your being here will cause division in the African church." Roy and Magaline listened. Then we all knelt and prayed together. In a matter of weeks, Calvin was up at the district office again and the commissioner informed him that Mrs. Hoops was in the government hospital for gall bladder surgery.

Cal came home and said, "Come on, Martie, we're going to visit her."

Alone in the hospital, Magaline was so glad they had come. Then the Bralliers invited Roy to bring their children over to stay with them while their mother was hospitalized and invited him to eat his evening meals with them. Martha made a special dinner at which she lit candles and served the meal very graciously. Years later Roy reminded her of the candles she had on the table.

He often remarked that this was the opening of the door that led them to the Church of God mission. He and Magaline gave many years before his death, both at Mwihila and in Tanzania. Magaline is still serving in Tanzania.

Calvin was like that. A deeply consecrated Christian, he was quiet, fearless, and direct. His words were few, but when an issue was involved, he never backed down, and when he spoke, people listened. They were great friends.

The Bralliers' fourth child, Janet, was born. She was a darling baby. This seemed the perfect family; everyone had so much love for the others. What a beautiful example of Christian love to present to the Kenya families. It was just ideal in every way.

But tragedy struck when Martha went into the bedroom one day to pick up little Janet only to discover that the child had died of crib death. It was a heart-breaking experience for this beautiful, young family. The experience was so astounding and so sudden that all of us shared the paralysis that seemed to hold our little mission family in its grip.

Calvin and Martha felt the need for privacy, and only after a night away from the tragedy could they bring themselves to open the door to the African family. As they did, the first one to come was one of Calvin's team of supervisors, Mr. Daniel Wako. Silently, but in a positive manner, he offered his condolences. "I know how you feel, for I have lost two children." One by one they came and shared grief experiences that they, too, had gone through. Of this Martha wrote,

*Healing came to me from those African people telling me that they had lost two or three or even five children, that they had been there, too, and that there was a oneness with us, for surely during those times the Lord was especially with us. They knew how to comfort us.*

*The scripture I learned as a little child was a special comfort to me as I lay awake at night: "He, watching over Israel, slumbers not or sleeps." David Livingston came down one*

*morning to visit us and we got down on our knees and prayed and wept together. Not more than two months later their little baby, Susie, was born prematurely, and we all brought our hot water bottles to make an incubator for her, but she was not able to survive. Then we were able to comfort them, for we had been there.*

This difficult experience endeared Calvin and Martha to the African community, for in a land in which so many children die, their very painful experience would enable them to minister to others in grief.

**Fear of Snakes**

Martha had to bring herself to overcome the fear of snakes at Ingotse. Her children learned to walk there and she was terrified by the many snakes. Finally, she just knelt and asked the Lord to deliver her from that fear. She told the Lord that this was their world and she did not want to raise children who were afraid of their world. She asked the Lord to remove that fear, and he did.

After the Schwiegers went on furlough, the Bralliers moved to Ingotse with Jane Ryan, the nurse. She and Martha worked very closely together, and one of their first projects was a daily vacation Bible school. The African children enjoyed it greatly and came out in great numbers. One of the activities the children enjoyed were the Sunday school leaflets that had been sent from the United States. The children had so few pictures in their homes and each one became a coveted possession on the wall of some hut. It was an opportunity of testimony to the many people of the village who entered the hut.

Steve was born while they lived at Ingotse. Before Michael had been born, a bus crosswise in the road, stuck in a foot of mud, made it impossible for them to pass on Martha's way to the hospital. Now with the birth of Steven imminent, the bridge had collapsed shortly after they arrived at Ingotse, and they would have to detour at least forty miles, partly through a corn field, to reach the main road, then another forty miles to the hospital in Kisumu. So fearing they would be unable to make it on time, Calvin and Martha went ahead of time to the Kisumu hotel to wait the arrival of their child. Jane Ryan stayed behind with Michael.

When Steven was six months old, he was hospitalized so ill that they feared for his life. They were greatly relieved when after much prayer the baby recovered.

### A Glimpse into the Family Life

Martha relates:

*Cal's work brought him home every night. All the children would line up at the window and wait for daddy. Then came the rush as they all flew into his arms for his kiss. Every evening we sat with the kids and sang and prayed. From the very beginning, as I tucked the small ones into bed, I'd bow my head and say, "Thank you, Jesus." From the beginning our children knew we loved the Lord and God loved them.*

*The missionaries were all so good in relating to our children. Frank took the boys to the Luanda shops and while they were driving along amidst the odor of spices, dried fish, and all the other smells of Asian cooking, Michael said, "Uncle Frank, I think I smell something."*

*"You do, Mike?"*

*"Yeah, I smell something."*

*Then Steve piped up, "I do, too, Uncle Frank. It has a candy smell." Frank laughed. They had been taught never to ask for anything, but they were using kid's psychology.*

### Sales

When the missionaries were ready to go home, they usually held a rummage sale. Mike and Steve became very much fascinated by the sales and thought they might try to sell their mother's best shoes. Martha wore an 8AA heel and AAAA toe—unusual sizes to replace—and had a year remaining until furlough. Without asking, the boys found their mother's shoes and took them out along the road where the people passed, set up their stand, and sold mama's shoes. They put the money in a small cup behind them, but when they reached for it later, it was missing.

When Jewell Hall heard about the transaction she was anxious to talk to Mike. "Mike," she asked, "what did your mother say when you sold her shoes?"

"Oh, Aunt Jewell. When my mother gets so mad she never says anything."

"And what did your dad say?"

"He wasn't as mad as mom, but I could tell by his eyes that he wasn't smiling."

### Holidays and Special Days

With a large group of young children on the mission, we could never forget the important holidays the children missed being away from their homeland. The parents and other staff members always entered into their holidays with as much enthusiasm as the children.

Christmas was a big celebration for the children. All the parents attended the main Christmas service at the different mission stations and then returned to the home of the Christmas hostess for the biggest and best Christmas party ever enjoyed. There may have been a Christmas play for the children, or just a Christmas story. Then after a sumptuous meal, Santa brought out the gifts.

One year David Gaulke dressed up as Santa, and with all the children around him as Santa's helpers running in all directions, distributing gifts to their moms, dads, aunties, and uncles, he said, "David Gaulke," and handed a parcel to Michael Brallier. It was then that the children knew David Gaulke was Santa, for no one could find him in the audience.

After the school for the missionary children opened at Mwihila and they were no longer required to make their journey several hundred miles from home, we were able to spend more time with them. There were three Brallier children, three Yutzys, four Richardsons, three Goodricks, and perhaps a few others whose names I do not remember. It was so refreshing to have the children with us.

A very strong bond existed between the Brallier family and the Donohews. The children had grown up to call Mr. Donohew "Uncle Big Donnie." In later years when the Bralliers moved to Vancouver, Washington, they moved across the river from Portland where the Donohews lived, and they continued the family relationship. Calvin was with Wick Donohew quite a bit of the time during Wick's hospitalization before his death. When he died, seventh-grade Michael was greatly grieved at the loss of his friend.

# Chapter 39

# The African Womens Society

As Nora Schwieger, Irene Engst, and I worked with the women in the hospital, dispensary, and maternity ward, we did not take long to sense their need for help. Practically all the women of the older generation had never had the opportunity of attending school. They had spent their time toiling in the gardens with their short-handled hoes, digging and cultivating their crops.

The people's lives had been regulated by local tradition. Each age and sex had special duties to carry out at definite times and circumstances. The men did some of the heavy work, but the women prepared the soil and grew the crops. They married at young ages and began bearing children every eighteen months to two years until menopause.

Life was hard and inconvenient. Grain had to be ground between two stones, water was carried great distances from the community spring, wood and sticks for fires had to be gathered; their lives were filled with extremely difficult work. Each week they walked many miles to the market to trade for a few cents for the family's meat, sugar, and tea.

Now that education was being introduced, the children, who had traditionally helped the mothers, were spending their daytime hours at school instead, placing more pressures on the women. They had to work even harder to obtain the extra money required for school fees and school uniforms.

In spite of their difficult task, women were the faithful participants of the church.

Mabel Baker had a Dorcas Society that had met regularly for many years. She taught them to sew and knit. They made many garments for the poor and needy and sold others to get money for their benevolent treasury.

As replacements came to the different mission stations for hospital work, we were released to do the work we had hoped to do for a long time. At that time missionary societies were forming in our villages. The women wanted to sew, but they had never had the opportunity to learn. The beginners started with the postcard-size quilt patches the women from the United States had cut out for us. Rita Ayanga and I would cut out small children's garments before class for the more experienced ones to sew. Rita also helped put backings on the baby quilts that they had joined together.

The proceeds were used for various missionary efforts, the first project being new windows and doors at the first school church at Ibeno, Kisii. Here was an opportunity to do real mission work among a group of people who spoke a different language and belonged to a different tribe.

They had heard of the great need in this area after a number of the Kisii had attended a revival meeting in Waluka, one of their Bunyore villages.

Not only was an outreach program needed, but the women needed a greater knowledge of the word of God. Only a few of them had gone very far in school, and their reading ability was limited. Bible classes appeared to be an urgent need. So we began with the Gospels. Rita Ayanga went with me as my interpreter, for although I used Luyia for everyday conversation, my confidence had not covered a Bible lesson. After a few lessons, the women asked me to try the Luyia. "You can do it, for we will help you." And that they did. I think one of the greatest hindrances to learning a language is the fear of making mistakes. They often corrected me as I spoke, and I smiled and went on. How considerate they were, and at no time was I ever ill at ease with them. When understanding and love are present, a person can do almost anything.

We went to individual villages at first, with varying results. The ones nearer the mission had been exposed to missionaries and were much more responsive. They tried to keep a schedule, but the more distant ones found the regularity of a program a bit more difficult to follow. Many times I would wait for an hour before they began to gather. I needed patience! I believe that patience is a God-given virtue that is doled out in very small quantities and has to be learned, with frequent refresher courses. Since I enjoyed knitting, I took it along to do while waiting, and the garment began to grow instead of an ulcer.

This was time consuming, and some other method would need to be used if we were to reach the majority of the women who needed help. So we chose several centers near enough for the women to walk and where several churches were close together. The women were happy to come together with another group. They enjoyed the social side of it as well as the teaching. Over the years we had studied nearly every book of the New Testament.

Then we began to organize. The pastor was usually the person to choose a responsible leader. The leaders came together on the mission and we began to make plans. A convention would give importance to our women's sessions. All of them liked the idea, for while the entire church had a convention held annually, many of them were unable to attend since they had never been chosen as delegates.

A delivery waiting room had been built by Mika Olubaya, one of the elders. Mika had always helped plan the large conventions in the past. When we asked if he would help us with our convention, he graciously accepted. A budget was needed to cover the expenses, for no funds were available for it. The menu would be very simple, but it would cost money. So we sat down and figured the amount it would cost to feed each woman for the three days they expected to attend the convention. If we could have it during the school holidays, we could possibly use the girls school or the Bible school facilities. We could allow two delegates from each village in addition to the district leader.

Mika Olubaya, Rita Ayanga, and I sat with the committee members and worked out the budget and menus. We would serve tea for breakfast, then the main meal at noon, and something not too heavy in the evening. We would need meat, corn meal, tea, sugar, bananas for cooking, sweet potatoes, greens, and the dark *obuli* [millet] flour that was preferred by the older women.

Perhaps they may add a few chickens. The group would include about three-hundred hungry people. Mika was a genius with crowds. I helped him haul the food, but he had to have utensils in which to cook all of this. So they found a fifty-gallon oil drum and cut it in two, yielding two fine pots to cook over the three stones that made their stove. They constantly fired it between the stones. No one bothered about the smoke. That made it taste more African. A large amount of wood was needed to keep the fire going continuously for the group. A wagonload of wood had to be found and purchased. Mika had authority to manage the money that they would send in prior to their coming. He employed all the helpers and took entire charge of the catering. All the money came on time. This was a special occasion and no one wanted to chance missing it.

At last the time came for the convention. Women came from every direction carrying their suitcases and blankets on their heads. There was a great handshaking as people met. This was the greatest occasion many of them had ever attended. To think they were getting to meet women from as far away as Ingotse, or Idakho, or Kima. It was like going to Nairobi. They belonged to something far greater than the little association of their village or district. They were making new friends.

This began a real time of spiritual growth for the women. Time after time, they knelt at the altar to pray for the strength of endurance. Wives prayed whose husbands had taken a second wife and who were compelled to leave their house and turn it over to a younger second, third, or fourth wife. It took more grace than the missionary working here had ever experienced. How can an inexperienced person give this poor soul guidance? Here was where her fellow worker came to the rescue. Those who passed through the same dilemma and could still bear witness to the power of God knew her heartaches and sorrows. They alone could help her bear her burden and, through prayer, leave her a stronger Christian ready to stand more hardships.

With the word of God in her favor, she took courage and renewed her faith, ready to face and even love the younger woman as a part of her extended family.

The Church of God Women became a strong organization. When the work began at Ibeno, Kisii, the women planned for their second project to build a temporary dispensary at Kisii for their newfound friends and Christians there. In addition to their sewing, they accepted talent money and began increasing it with various forms of trading. By the time the building was ready to be built, they had given two-thousand shillings (about four-hundred dollars).

When I left on furlough in 1961, Lydia Hansen and Rita carried on the Women's work in the Bunyore area. When I remained at home instead of returning, Irene Engst took over the Bunyore societies in addition to the ones she had at Mwihila. Rita worked with her in the same manner that she worked with me.

Then when Nora Schwieger retired, Irene handled her societies in addition to the ones that I had at Bunyore. She and Rita worked very faithfully together.

After I retired, the womens conference room in the nursery school building was taken for use as a Bible school classroom, and the church allocated the women the two northwest corners of the Kima church for a chapel and workroom.

Unknown to me, they had dedicated the chapel to me because I had begun the womens society in Bunyore. Five years later, when I married and returned to Kima with Edgar Williams, he suggested that the name be changed to Lima Williams. But that is how the women knew me, and to them I would always be Miss Lehmer. They always managed to call me Mrs. Williams with the first handshake, but after that I was Miss Lehmer again.

In fact, they really initiated Edgar to the tribe by requesting a dowry. They said I was their girl and had come to them as a very young person, and he must pay a dowry. They made an elaborate wedding feast for us and invited all the important leaders of the church. Before the group, Edgar complied and gave them the price of a cow and a goat, presented by his chaplain, Hezeron Marisia. From that time on he was their brother-in-law.

When we left to retire, one of the missionary presidents invited us to come to their church and speak about the family. After we had eaten a delicious lunch of chicken and *obusuma*, several of the women invited Edgar and me into one of the adjoining rooms, drew back a curtain, and displayed a Singer sewing machine. They said to their brother-in-law, Edgar, "We want you to see what we bought with our share of your dowry. We put the money out for talent money and we worked until we were able to buy this sewing machine. Now it will be easier to make garments than it was by hand. Thank you again and God bless you."

Each district divided the money and used it as they saw fit, but Kima will always remember the event. And we will always remember them.

After Lydia Hansen returned from furlough in 1962, she resumed the womens society and nursery school responsibilities that I had assumed formerly. Mrs. Rita Ayanga was still with her.

With the advance program of the Bible school needing more classroom space, the three-room building used by the nursery school and the womens conference room and work area could well have been the answer. The nursery school had served the neighborhood children for twenty-five years and had now overflowed into the surrounding communities where similar institutions had been started by the local congregations. This had been its purpose from the beginning.

The women were offered facilities in the north wing of the church for a chapel and workroom where they could still function. Lydia Hansen relates the change:

*The women's workroom and conference hall were moved into the north wing of the church. The first service held in the Lima Lehmer chapel was a staff devotional meeting during which two of the mission babies were dedicated. Doug Welch presided over that meeting.*

*I can't begin to tell how much I, as well as many others before and after me, depended on Rita Ayanga. She had been trained as a midwife by Lima Lehmer in the first nursing class, later as a nursery school teacher, then as a Bible teacher and translator. She worked with all the missionaries and translated songs, scriptures, and Sunday school lessons in the services. Mabel Baker often used Rita in translation work. After Irene Engst came to Kima, Rita and she worked together in the womens society. When Irene left for home, the assembly provided Rita with transportation and she worked in the villages alone. She was a person with a rare gift of humor, and our work would have been greatly handicapped without her. Since her passing, she is greatly missed.*

## Chapter 40

# Rev. Rita
# Paulo Ayanga

**R**ita Paulo was an African young woman who came to work at the hospital and to train as a midwife in 1937. She must have been about sixteen years old, a typical giggly teenager, full of fun. When she finished her training and received government recognition, she became an employee of the maternity hospital, and worked there with me for the next fifteen years. I can only praise Rita for her work. She was dependable, efficient, good natured, and, above all else, a sincere Christian. From an early age, she taught a Sunday school class on the mission. When the nursery school began, she was in charge of it for the most part. She helped train teachers, cared for the children, made their uniforms, and taught them songs and Bible stories, in addition to delivering babies as the mothers came to the hospital. Everyone loved her. When I went to the villages, she accompanied me and helped with the language. We learned together, for her English and my Olunyore were scanty when she first came.

When I left for furlough in 1944, Twyla Ludwig put Rita in charge of the maternity hospital. By this time she was able to handle normal deliveries and to identify abnormal ones in the prenatal clinic.

While I was home, she became engaged to and married John Ayanga, the son of an Anglican padre. Rita loved her work and told John she would marry him but she wanted to stay with the mission and could not go to his village to live. John was a very good-natured African and let her break the native custom. They set up housekeeping in a small house on the mission and lived there until she retired forty years later. John was a tailor and went back and forth to his work every morning and evening on his bicycle.

By the time I returned from my long furlough, Rita had a little girl she had named Lima. After that, she had seven more children.

Rita was a very progressive young woman. She became interested in Bible work and attended one or two classes with the men students at the Bible school. Oftentimes she would say to me, "I've been born before my time." She envied the young women who were able to go on to high school and make a place for themselves in the field of education. Although she was never able to achieve the goal she would have been qualified to achieve, she saw to it that all of her children received a good education; one even did graduate work.

After we began the womens society work among the Bunyore churches, Rita went with me and we worked together in the villages. She and I helped the women with their sewing. As our Bible classes developed, Rita became quite efficient as a Bible teacher. Sometimes when I went to Kisii, she took over the classes for me. The one problem was that of transportation, and it was not until after Irene Engst left that the African Assembly was able to provide her with a car to do the womens society work.

She was well known throughout the womens society circles in Kenya, for she had helped with the town societies on many occasions. In 1960, when the Womens World Day of Prayer celebrated its seventy-fifth anniversary in Ndola, Northern Rhodesia, Rita was chosen to represent all the churches of Kenya as Kenya's delegate. The women had chosen one woman from each country of Africa south of the Sahara Desert. It was a rich experience for her and we were very proud of her. She made many friends at Ndola, including the wife of the president of Nigeria.

After giving forty-five years to the mission, Rita retired and finally began building her home in her husband's village. Her husband, John, had now finished Bible school and had become an Anglican padre. After retiring, Rita had begun helping

John with his church work. She was on her way to Nairobi for a meeting with a group of other people when she met with a fatal automobile accident.

The church assembly was planning a very large retirement celebration for her that had not yet transpired. They had obtained a cow and some furniture for her as an appreciation gift, and they were saddened to be unable to present them to her. The gifts had to be given instead to the Ayanga family in her memory.

Rita's daughter, Hazel, who is now a librarian in the university library in Nairobi, wrote of her mother in such endearing terms and expressed her desire to write a book titled *Laughing Mother*. That was typical of Rita. She was one of the happiest, kindest, and most versatile persons I have ever worked with. I often felt as if we imposed on her, for many times when the various missionaries needed an interpreter on short notice, we asked Rita to accompany us to a village on Sunday, her day off, and she graciously went.

Rita gave more time than any missionary ever gave to our work there, and her influence reached much farther. I was told that several thousand people attended her funeral. Everyone loved Rita, because she loved everyone, but above all, she led so many of them to God, helped them in their sorrows, and shared their joys and trials. Although she was a Kisa girl, she soon became a part of the Bunyore tribe due to the assistance she gave them. Other women will be raised up to fill useful places in Kenya, but no one will ever fill the place she made for her beloved people.

# Chapter 41

# Hazel McDilda

## (1951-1961)

**H**azel McDilda has shared a few memories of her work as a surgical nurse at Mwihila:

*On my first night at Kima, I stayed with Mabel Baker and remained with her until Lydia's house was finished. They were remodeling it at the time. Mabel Baker came into the dark bedroom and gave me a flashlight. She flashed the light on the ceiling and said, "Now dearie, do you see those little tails hanging down there?"*

*"Yes," came out very cautiously.*

*"Now don't worry. Those are just little lizards and they won't hurt you; they'll stay right up there."*

*I wouldn't have noticed if she hadn't shown me, but every once in a while, I flashed the light on the ceiling to see if they were still there. I scarcely slept that night, but before long I stopped that foolishness, for she knew what she was talking about. She was just a dear.*

*In a day or so, Lydia took me to the maternity hospital where a patient was in labor.*

*"Okay, Hazel, she's all yours," she said.*

*I had never done a delivery, so I said, "I'll observe and let the African nurses deliver this one. I will see how they do it." I was very scared. Everyone is, for there are so many things to do that you have never done before. You just have to remember that God has called you and he will help you, and he always does.*

*On New Year's Eve, Lydia and I decided to liven up the mission at Kima, so we stayed up until the New Year had come in and then we took the pressure lamp and went down to the church and rang the bell. We went to Donohews' next, and Wick Donohew, hearing the church bell, got up thinking it meant a fire on the mission compound. Next we went to Bralliers', but awoke the youngsters and by the time they were quieted down, the parents were in no festive mood. Before leaving the house, we had filled our Thermos with hot water and gone to Mabel Baker's house. Being British, a cup of tea is always acceptable, so she arose, pulled out the cookies, and we celebrated with a tea party. Those are just a few of the personal experiences we have always cherished.*

*The time had come for Irene Engst to go on furlough, so I was sent to Mwihila to live with Jewell and to help at the dispensary. The dispensary was small, but it provided an excellent opportunity to initiate our creative ability in making croup tents and improvised incubators for the premature infants. They weren't as good as those in the States, but they helped.*

Each day brought new experiences for Hazel. Frank LaFont was building the new teacher's house for Jewell and Irene across the river on the school compound at Mwilila. He needed water for the concrete floor they were laying, but he did not have time to drive the truck and wait until the men filled the sixty-gallon drums with water, so he asked Hazel if she would drive the truck to the river, leave it while the men filled the drums, and then drive it to the house under construction. The dispensary had a line of people, so when they told her that all the drums were filled, she ran down, drove the truck, and went back to her patients. This went on for two or three days until they had all the water needed for that part of the building.

The dispensary building, so very useful in Irene's early days of treating patients, was beginning to be too small, old, and rat infested. Or was it that the new missionaries were shocked at such simple beginnings after leaving their modern hospitals in the homeland? Perhaps, but not entirely, for when a rat jumped out on the shoulder of the new doctor's wife, pandemonium broke loose. Elsie Gaulke and the other nurses screamed. The rats were quite disturbed at losing their quiet attendant, Irene, to this group of loudly laughing, excited nurses sharing their new experiences. Then to add to it, the doctor came in and worked there, too. No wonder the dispensary had suddenly shrunk in size. The rats often sat on the ledge on the top of the wall and eyed the new occupants as if to say, "Don't come any closer."

The greatest day finally came when they were able to move into the new dispensary. The new building was separated into wards, laboratory, pharmacy, and an operating room. Although small and inconvenient, it was used until the second building was built.

How thankful they were to be in the new buildings. Though they seemed at first to prove sufficient, before long it was again too small for our needs.

When the David Gaulkes arrived in 1953, they lived with the Yutzys while their house was under construction. Then when Vera Martin came, she and Hazel McDilda lived with the Gaulkes until their house was completed. Housing usually required a time of shifting until a family or individual had been settled in. With the new hospital and its large staff coming, a busy building program was in operation on both sides of the river. The teacher training center, too, was in an expansion program as new teachers houses and classrooms were added. Mwihila was fast becoming a small village, with a great number of occupants.

Hazel relates some of her early hospital experiences with the Gaulkes:

*The Gaulkes demanded the best of you but never made you feel that you had to do it. They often made comments to us nurses on how much they appreciated the fact that we maintained our professional status and always were careful about our uniforms.*

*One thing we appreciated about David Gaulke was his sympathetic attitude with the nurses. We knew we were not capable of treating patients beyond what we were trained to do. Yet the doctor realized that he couldn't see every patient. He would give us instructions and was very patient with our questions. If we happened to make a wrong diagnosis or did something wrong, he never became upset or quarreled with us; he just helped us so that it would never happen again. He was terribly overworked himself, as were all of us.*

*We used the laboratory for our operating room before the*

main hospital operating room was in use. The doctor suggested that our first operation should be a simple one rather than a borderline case, for if it were not successful, the patients would be afraid to come. Fortunately the first was successful.

He was an excellent surgeon, always considerate of the patient and honest with himself. All the surgeries were begun with prayer and the operating room seemed hallowed by the presence of God.

Nearly every time Dr. Gaulke would go to Kisii or the other dispensaries, we seemed to receive the most difficult cases. One time an obstetrical case was brought in with a prolapsed arm. We didn't know what to do. Vera and I worked with her and there was just no possibility of getting her to another doctor, for it was raining and the muddy roads were impassable. We took her into the operating room, worked and prayed, did what we had been taught to do, and everything worked out very well. We had a live baby. When the doctor came back, two excited nurses related the story to him and asked him what they should have done. Then he returned the question and asked them what we had done. When we told him, he said, "That is exactly what you should have done." He just looked at us and shook his head, saying, "Someone must have been watching over you because that would have been a difficult delivery for me."

Our patient clinic was large. Many times one hundred fifty patients would arrive in a morning. The doctor could not possibly see all of them. Each of us had an assignment. The one in charge of the clinic would examine the patients and treat them, referring all the difficult patients to the doctor.

I assisted the doctor in most of his surgeries before the other doctors came. Many times after opening a patient, he would say, "This is the most difficult part of my job—not having someone to help me make a decision. It's difficult to know what to do when you're alone." He would perform the surgery, and when he finished, he would turn over the instruments to me and say, "Okay, you can finish up and do the embroidery work," and I would finish suturing.

The Gaulkes loved animals. They had a boxer bulldog and had become very much attached to it. When they were ready to leave, they brought all the dog's equipment such as food and vitamins down to me and said, "He is now yours," and they both stood there and cried.

David always walked from his home to the clinic and, seeing a mangy old dog come up to him, he always stopped to pet it and proceeded to pick the ticks off its body. The children loved *him as well as the animals. At staff meetings, when the doctor would sit back in a secluded corner, glancing over a magazine he had not yet read, he was soon interrupted by several of the mission children bouncing up on his lap and calling him by their favorite name for him, "Big Bear." This was not only true on the mission, but also at resorts. He always had children around him.*

A number of years ago, before going to China, the Gaulkes were ready to adopt two children, but when the social workers learned of their commitment to mission service out of the country, they refused to allow the adoption to go through. It was always a disappointment to the Gaulkes, for they both loved children.

Hazel tells of his concern over the economic needs of the people during a famine:

*A twelve-year-old girl came to the clinic with a stick protruding from her leg. I removed it, treated the wound, and sent her home. Two or three days later she returned and said, "You didn't get rid of all the stick." Sure enough, there was another piece in the wound, so again I removed it. When she returned the third time with another piece of stick in the same place, Mr. Eliphas, our dispenser, came to me and said, "Miss McDilda, I have something to tell you about that case. This is famine time and the people do not have enough food. They know there will be food at the hospital and they will get their three meals a day. She is putting that stick in that sore so that she can be admitted to the hospital."*

*When the doctor heard the story, he said, "Admit her." During the famine, he was always helping the people, especially the families of the hospital employees, for they couldn't afford to pay black-market prices for the flour that they used.*

*The Gaulkes were wonderful people. Sometimes we got uptight with him, but after all, he probably had reason to get upset with us, too. Elsie was always gentle, but firm. She was a perfectionist in her work, but not in an objectionable manner.*

The Gaulkes both liked good things—good clothes, a good home, good food—and she was an excellent housekeeper. Yet for the sake of the gospel, they adapted themselves to the surroundings as we will see later on.

## Chapter 42

# The Yutzys Come to Mwihila

On October 4, 1952, James and Glenna Yutzy arrived in Mwihila with their four-month-old daughter Donna to work in the teacher traning center. They shared the only house on the mission with Jewell Hall until a new one could be built for her on the government property across the river.

Jim and Glenna's first assignment was the training of the choirs both for the coming school competition and for the church choirs as they participated in their Christmas programs. James soon found plenty of activity in hauling supplies for the new permanent buildings.

Mabel Baker taught them language study at Kima. James, Glenna, and Velma Schneider seemed to take it very seriously under such an efficient teacher. Glenna found it more difficult since she had a four-month-old baby to care for, but gradually as Donna's equipment arrived about six months later, she was easier to care for.

James became principal when Jewell went home on furlough. Glenna said of Jewell,

*How we depended on Jewell. She was like a mother to us young ones; she had so much experience and we were so young*

169

*and green; she was so willing to share and help us through any problems we might have. The first term only Irene, Jewell, and we were involved in the school and so we learned to depend on each other; we became very close.*

They soon adjusted to living without conveniences and with only a truck trip every two weeks to Kisumu for groceries and supplies. Then they would go to the pool for a swim and picnic, which was a treat.

They soon became good friends with the Africans whom they learned to love very much. But this presented quite a problem when the time came to select a new class. A limited number of places were available, and it was hard to resist the pleas of the students to be admitted. Yet standards had to be maintained.

The teacher training center was a boarding school and required constant supervision. But the problems were minimal in comparison with those in the United States. Daily chapel classes were held. James taught Bible, music, and math courses. Jewell and James were very concerned for their students that they would make a proper showing during their examination time.

Glenna found herself busy as the mission bookkeeper, working under Wick Donohew. A. F. Gray set up the books and trained Glenna when she first arrived and lived at Kima. Monthly reports were sent to the Missionary Board. She ran the short-wave radio three times a day to the other stations, collected the money for the Mwihila station, kept books for the school that had to be audited by the government, and was the official hostess for all the mission guests. She enjoyed the latter very much.

Then the Gaulkes came to live with the Yutzys until their house was built. By this time Jewell and Irene were living in the new house supplied for them by the government. In 1954, Glenna gave birth to a daughter, Linda, assisted by the Gaulkes. Six years later, their son, Jerry, was born. He was delivered by Dr. Smith and Delores Beatty. It is really convenient to have doctors and nurses so near to care for your needs.

While Glenna was busy as a housewife, full-time mother, and missionary, James was using his electrical engineering training in the tremendous building program that was mushrooming at Mwihila. He soon had water and electricity in the first mission house and was wiring the units in the teacher training center, teachers' houses, and dormitories. The hospital was progressing under the leadership of Frank LaFont, and

James became the maintenance man and electrician on the station.

While skilled manual services were in demand, they did not neglect the spiritual demands of the outlying churches. James worked with the local pastors, conducting classes once a week with them. He taught them tithing and how to keep books for the local congregations by helping them balance their books each month. When Cal Brallier went on furlough, James took over his job as area superintendent for all of the Church of God school. Then about 1960, the teacher training center was beginning to change into a high school. As the class graduated, a new high school class was begun and eventually the teacher training was eliminated in favor of the high school for boys.

With still some time left from a busy schedule, James became the area scouting commissioner with about one hundred troops.

They needed a school for the twelve mission children who were now available in the three stations. It would be a much more economical matter than to send them to a boarding school two hundred fifty miles away. At that time a small one-room school was built on the mission side of the river where the children could attend with the leadership of an American teacher. Miss Vivian Phelps came and set up the school and taught the children to the sixth grade. The school was named Baker Elementary School in honor of Mabel Baker, who had served so faithfully for thirty-nine years and who had now retired to her home in South Africa.

Here many of our mission children were able to attend school without going so far away from home and were able to spend more time with their parents.

We are very much indebted to Glenna Yutzy, who shared the following report with us concerning the activities of her late husband, James. She had the privilege of going to Kenya to visit the work she and her husband did so much to promote during their eleven years there. She ended by saying:

*We did have happy years serving the Lord, living a regular family life in another country. And when it was time for us to return to the United States for good, it was hard to leave all that we had come so close to there for eleven years. It was not easy to tell them all good-bye and start a new life in the United States, but the Lord helped us make the adjustment. We did not return with a large bank account, but we had a rich life and so many memories and friends. Hardly a day goes by that we do not think of something that happened in Kenya. It was such a great part of our life.*

In speaking of returning to Kenya in 1983, she said,

*I slipped away from the tour group to the school side and took pictures of our home and school. The school has grown; there are four hundred students attending there now. I was pleased with what I saw. It was the best therapy I could have done for myself, to go back and hear the Africans still talking about James.*

*James and I, and I am sure you, too, and all the other missionaries, felt the same way, that our goal was to work ourselves out of a job. Well, returning after twenty years, I was so happy to see the work of the church, Sunday school, women's work, choirs, education, scouting, medical and administration all being done by the African people themselves. I am sure the late Wick Donohew, Herman Smith, Mabel Baker, the Gaulkes, Jewell Hall, Roy Hoops, James, and all the others who have gone to heaven are all looking down giving their approval. Praise the Lord!*

**Chapter 43**

# The Work Advances at Mwihila Hospital

Vera Martin arrived in October 1954 with Hazel McDilda. Vera had wanted to be a missionary from the time she was a small child. After studying nursing at Anderson College, she took additional work in administering anesthesia. As the women traveled the dusty road to Kenya, they were greeted along the way from Kakamega to Mwihila by groups from a number of churches along the way singing to welcome the missionaries. Another group awaited their arrival at the church at Mwihila. Vera noticed one woman in the crowd who stood out for her beauty. Her name was Stella and she was a teacher. She was not only beautiful, but talented and became Vera's interpreter of both language and customs during her first few months there.

The hospital setup was not according to the American idea of good nursing procedures. The delivery room and the dispensary were together. No infected patients ever came into the delivery room, but the lack of buildings and space in this setting changed many of her preconceived notions. Soon she, too, began using the Dettol bottle (Britain's disinfectant) generously to remove any hidden germs that might be lurking in a secluded spot. As a result no obstetrical case became septic.

## Plans for a Hospital

Dr. Gaulke had drawn the plans for the hospital project as he and James Yutzy sat around their dining room table. Frank LaFont was getting the raw materials ready to begin the project, but it had to be very carefully planned before any activity could take place. Elsie Gaulke and Vera Martin made several trips to visit other hospitals in Kenya with training schools in order to get practical ideas for an African operated hospital. Each one differed according to staff, equipment, and location. These new nurses just fresh from the United States were shocked to find two patients in a bed, wrapped in sheets in a manner that kept them from touching. They probably used a similar method as their patient load increased, since it doubled the bed space. It was far better than having the patient sleeping under the bed as was found some places.

David and Elsie Gaulke planned very wisely in their building program. They were able to use the little metal dispensary for more than a year while Frank LaFont built the permanent building for emergency surgery and a laboratory. Several rooms in the second building later became the laboratory and classroom for nurses. The nurses' dormitory was the next most important building, for unless nurses were trained, they would not be able to handle the large hospital load of patients when it was finally opened. Then came the construction of the main hospital building.

One of the important posts was that of a trained dispenser. They soon found Elifaz, who had worked for years on one of our neighboring missions and later went to Nairobi to work. He was a good Christian, gentle, yet firm, in dealing with the people, honest, faithful, and accurate with accounts.

Vera relates her first surgical case:

*Our first surgical case was one of our missionaries, Nora Schwieger, who had to have emergency surgery. This was also my first time to give ether by the drip method rather than by machine. My knees turned to water with fear of giving too much ether to the patient. If I gave her too little, she could kick, but if too much, she wouldn't feel like kicking. The doctor said, "She needs to be deeper." Ruben, her husband, was standing by during the operation and when the doctor asked for the suction, Ruben, in his helpful manner, reached right over the sterile section and nearly touched the sterile area. Dr. Gaulke said, "Ruben, we don't want you touching anything." Nora came through all right.*

174

## Beginning of the Nursing School

*Elsie Gaulke was soon able to begin the nursing school. She was excellent and yet strict, but was respected by the students. She spoke only once and they understood. We tried to use students who had finished the eighth grade because they had to have some knowledge of English. There were no medical books in their language. We taught them medical subjects as well as English since both were needed.*

*At first we took only girls but later learned that we needed male orderlies, so we built them a mud hut with a concrete floor for their dormitory. Twenty students were in the first class. After that we took in fewer. Some of them were eliminated because they were unable to pass the hospital examinations, and if they were unable to pass our exams, we did not want them to sit for the government exams. We discouraged repeaters, for there were plenty of good students waiting to enter. It was a two-year program and would be equivalent to the practical nurse's degree in the United States. However, we gave them more training than would be given a practical nurse, such as training in how to give IVs and deliver babies. Obstetrics was not included in the Kenya licensed course but was approved for us as a special concession since Naomi Sweeney was on our staff. Naomi had trained as a midwife in England before coming to Kenya.*

During this time Vera Martin was elected to be on the Medical Council of Kenya, which included all the government and mission hospitals. She sat on the licensing board for four years to review nurses who entered the colony for registration. Through the contacts she made, our mission received many extra considerations such as the food programs for the three mission stations. They gave us free food for the needy people supplied by some of the benevolent agencies from America and other countries. They received yellow cornmeal, though it did not gain acceptance among the people; they thought we fed that only to the cattle. However, they enjoyed white cornmeal, oil, and butter. They were not accustomed to cheese and did not acquire the taste for it. Several free medications were made available—inoculations for DPT (diptheria, tetanus, whooping cough), measles, and polio. Clinics were set up in different villages to administer the inoculations.

## Vera Martin speaks of the Gaulkes

Vera Martin knew the Gaulkes well and has written of her affection for them:

The David Gaulkes were the nicest people and demanded efficiency. They were very knowledgeable and expected everyone else to be the same. Dr. Gaulke used to say, "You don't have to know as much as I do, but almost as much." He had a hearing problem that he felt resulted from his medications for malaria. But he always heard what he wanted to hear! One day when Princess Margaret came to Kenya, I wanted the nurses to have the opportunity of meeting a part of the royal family since they were British subjects. A week before I told the doctor that we would be going; in fact, I told him several times. He didn't say yes or no. So we all dressed in uniform and went to Kisumu to see Princess Margaret.

When we got there, they asked for our tickets. I explained that I didn't even know that tickets were necessary, but I had brought my nurses to see Princess Margaret. There was no problem; they put us right up in the front row behind the chiefs, the best place possible. We had an enjoyable day. When we returned to the mission about 6 P.M., he was infuriated. He had had a surgical emergency and was upset that the anesthetist had gone. I was angry at him, too, for I had told him in advance that we were going. He said, "I didn't hear you" and I told him he didn't listen. I understood why he was upset, but I'm glad we went. We really had a good time.

In 1955 Merlene Huber came as our lab technician. She spent two terms teaching three young men each term the laboratory work. Merlene was a gifted musician and often played for our services. She loved to go to the villages for services.

Naomi Sweeney also came in 1955. She had trained as a midwife in England on her way to Kenya, so she greatly enhanced the nursing program. She was our linguist; both Luyia and Swahili became second nature to her. Some of us learned enough to get by, but Sweeney would go out and teach a Sunday school class without an interpreter. She had no inhibitions with the language. If she made a mistake and the Africans laughed at it, she laughed with them. Nothing ever bothered her.

Hazel McDilda was an excellent nurse and a hard worker. She was not afraid to tackle anything, but she suffered at times from ill health. Malaria got her down, and then she had an intestinal abnormality that required immediate surgery at home. So she was flown to the United States. Hazel served two terms on the field.

Delores Beatty was a general nurse and taught in the nursing school.

*Cornelia Bartnett came to Kenya with a nursing degree. I was then in charge of the nursing school and since I am not a teacher, I was thrilled when she arrived. Besides her nursing degree, she had an additional two years of school, but she did not have practical work in nursing. Though she had never seen a delivery, she took over the nursing school one term.*

*Darlene Detwiler and Marlene Huber came to Kenya together. Darlene was an excellent nurse and became matron of the hospital. She served two terms and returned on several occasions to fill in during emergencies.*

*David Livingston was one of our prize possessions. When he first came, there was no place for his family to live at Mwihila, so they lived at Kima. He was in language study there. David Gaulke had a heavy work load at the hospital and wanted to train David Livingston every Tuesday and Thursday, so he set those two days aside for surgery only. David Livingston was a slow moving person. He would come in late for surgery nearly each day with a large map in his hand. "I've found a new way to get here today," he would say with his little chuckle, or "I had a flat tire," or "I was stuck in the mud." Dr. Gaulke was always punctual, so he didn't often wait.*

*Dr. Gaulke would say, "Well, you knew that. Why didn't you start earlier?" But they were good friends and worked well together.*

*Dr. Livingston did surgery with his eyes shut. He was the only doctor I ever knew who operated with his eyes shut. He'd have his hand inside the patient's abdomen and he would stand there—you didn't know if he was singing or quoting scripture, for he sang a lot when he was operating—and he'd feel the organs as he operated. He said that was the way he could see the whole pattern of everything; he knew the exact position of each organ.*

*I worked with him at Ingotse when he came every Monday. One patient came in with a track across its little buttocks and leg such as a mole would make in the ground. The mother said the baby cried all the time. When David saw it, he named some big fourteen syllable word and said, "Do you have some ethyl chlorine?"*

*Then he told me to spray some at each end of the track and anywhere there was an exit or entrance. I thought he was batty, but I did what he told me. When I saw him again I asked if he had ever seen this disease before. He had not, but he had remembered studying about it. It was caused by an insect like a little mite.*

*We all had great confidence in Dr. Livingston. He was one*

*of the kindest and most gentle persons we had ever met. Dr. Livingston certainly knew what he was doing. He was one of the happiest individuals, a wonderful linguist, good pianist, efficient in every area of his life. Above all, he was a dedicated Christian. We lost something when he left Africa, but he had a family of four children to educate. Joan Livingston was a nurse, too, though caring for their four children took most of her time while on the mission.*

*Other medical personnel were Richard and Donna Smith, a doctor and nurse team. Donna suffered frequent bouts of malaria while there. She was busy with the care of the children born there. Richard was a very good doctor. The Smiths left after their first term.*

*Dr. Harold LaFont was the son of Frank and Margaret LaFont. As a teen-ager he spent one term with his parents in Kenya, then returned to the United States for study. After marrying, they returned to Kenya for a term. He was a fine surgeon. They have four sons.*

*I met Roger and Margaret Bruce before retiring but did not get very well acquainted with them. Vera Martin lived at Ingotse for a while when Jane Ryan was on furlough; then after Jane married and returned to Kenya, Vera remained in charge of the dispensary at Ingotse.*

*The Mwihila hospital maintained a good evangelistic program. The staff endeavored to go to the villages for services whenever possible. Only emergency services were available at the hospital on Sundays.*

*Going to the villages on Sunday took most of the day. Many of the churches could not be reached by car, so it involved walking to the church from where the road ended, and then they always expected the guests to remain for dinner. It was necessary to have someone watch the car, for otherwise it may have been damaged.*

*Regular hospital services were held daily in the wards as well as for the outpatients. Mika Olubaya or Elifaz conducted them.*

How I appreciated Mika Olubaya when he was still at Kima. He had been a staunch supporter of the Kima hospital program for many years. In fact, he helped build the temporary maternity ward for us. Each year when we had our large convention for many years. In fact, he helped build the temporary maternity ward for us. Each year when we had our large convention meeting. He would always sit with us telling us how much meat, flour, sugar, tea, bananas, firewood, oil, and greens to buy. I'd turn the money over to him and he would buy the food, bring the cooks, be responsible for serving, and then put the mission back in order again when it was finished.

When they started the Mwilila Hospital and needed a trustworthy overseer for the responsibilities, I approached Mika. Formerly he had been giving his time voluntarily to the church, but with a growing family, he now needed remunerative work. He was very willing to go. I just do not know how we managed without him, but God sent us someone else.

Mika was in charge of our kitchen, buying foodstuffs, planning meals, and buying for the hospital. He oversaw the laundry. You can't imagine all the problems we had. He checked the linens as they went to the laundry and counted them when they came back.

One time our linens and medicines were being stolen. We finally had to call the police. In the suspected person's house, they found sheets, baby blankets, pillow slips, and other items—not half a dozen but perhaps a hundred or so pieces. So we had to dismiss that employee in spite of the fact that he was a likable person and good at his work.

Mika and Elifaz did shared responsibilities for the chapel. Both were among the finest of the African Christians. Mika was like Nathanael in the Bible—without guile. His wife, Joyce, was a most loving person. His son, Oliver Olubaya, was one of the first young people to go to Anderson College and he married Amelia Litondo.

Mwihila hospital was one of the most modern in Kenya Colony. It began with one hundred beds and was built in the form of an *H*. A fine laboratory, X-ray, and modern operating room were set up efficiently. It was dedicated in 1955 and named Nora Hunter Memorial Hospital. The Womens Missionary Society in America built the church at a cost of about one hundred twenty-five thousand dollars. Three doctors' homes and two nurses' duplexes were built on the hospital compound.

# Chapter 44

# Edna Thimes

Edna Thimes came to Kenya in 1960 and spent nineteen years in various phases of hospital work. Rather than duplicating other phases of hospital work, she will relate her experiences in more advanced methods of health care which in the early days would not have been available or acceptable. As health care and education advanced, so have health patterns. Many of the old taboos still exist, and yet the better-educated persons are eager to accept the new and modern methods.

One of the first problems Edna faced as she came to Kima was the transfer of certain buildings and land to the Bunyore Girls School. As the institution grew into a high school, more buildings were required. The government insisted that the buildings formerly used for the obstetrical ward, the public health facilities, kitchen, office, chapel, and the land become property of the girls school. After a reasonable settlement was made to replace the buildings, they were rebuilt near the hospital building.

When those buildings were built, no accurate long-range planning had been made, for no one knew that the girls school would develop into an institution of six-hundred girls. The former plan was for the development of the Kima Hospital; instead it went to Mwihila. Edna found herself with the problem of cramping the much-needed buildings into the small plot across the road from the girls school compound. In spite of the inconvenience of rebuilding, I am sure that it was much more convenient for the nurses.

Land has always been a problem at the Kima Mission, which is situated in the heart of one of the most populous tribes in North Nyanza. Kima itself looks like a small city, with its large church, three institutions, and housing for the personnel built on thirty-two acres.

Edna gives a report of her work while there:

*I was a public health nurse before I went to Kenya. We emphasized that it was better to prevent disease than to cure it. At that time practically all medical practice in Kenya was curative and not preventive. Almost all children in America were receiving immunizations for communicable diseases. This was not so in Kenya. We would purchase a few bottles of different kinds of vaccines and for a small charge give them to the children who were brought into our out-patient clinic. This simply was not adequate. Scores of children were being admitted to our hospitals with complications following childhood diseases. They were dying with meningitis, pneumonia, otitis media, and other complications of communicable diseases.*

*This challenged me to promote a program that would make immunizations against childhood diseases available for all children in our area. I searched long and hard for a charitable organization to finance such a program. OXFAM from England was interested in such a project. They paid for public health training for one of our nurses and built us a lovely building with a pavilion in which to conduct our clinics at Kima Hospital. The government provided us with free vaccines. The community still did not respond as we thought they would. They just could not understand how an injection or medicine dropped on the tongue could keep their children from having childhood diseases; they felt all children were supposed to have these diseases.*

*We needed something extra to entice the mothers to bring their children to the clinic for immunizations. After much pondering and searching, we were able to get powdered milk, corn meal, and cooking oil from UNICEF to give to every child who attended the clinic. Most of the children were malnourished and hungry, and so the food encouraged the mothers to bring their children to the clinic. This gave us the opportunity to weigh the children and teach the mothers how to care for them better, as well as to vaccinate them against childhood diseases and give them food. It was not long until our clinics at Kima Hospital were full and running over. This took care of the area within walking distance of Kima Hospital. But what about the rest of the eighty-one square mile area for which we were responsible? We presented the need of a mobile Public Health unit to OXFAM so that we could service all nine sublocations in our area. They bought us a car and provided us with another nurse so that we could have a mobile unit as well. The subchief in each sublocation provided us with a place to conduct our mobile clinics; sometimes it was a school, a church, or just under a tree. It was a thrill to see the people respond to preventive medicine. Polio and other child-hood diseases were practically wiped out in our location. Preventive medicine has caught on in all of Kenya now.*

*Another area that was practically untouched was family planning. It was not unusual for a woman to give birth to twelve to fifteen children with only about half of them sur-viving. She was never able to regain her strength between pregnancies; therefore, her babies were not strong and healthy when they were born. Many of the babies died before they were a year old. It was so important for them to space their children so that the mother would have time to regain her strength between pregnancies. It was not good for the family to have more children than they were able to care for. Family planning was very difficult to get across to the people due to their ideas about childbirth. Every time we got a group of women together at our well baby clinics and prenatal clinics, for instance, we gave lectures on family planning. Gradually it caught on.*

*Most of the women in Kenya deliver at home. If compli-cations occurred, they often died before they could get to a hospital. So many women died in their homes during child-birth.*

*This created another problem. If the mother died during childbirth, the new baby did not have a chance to survive unless an institution took the baby in. Larger hospitals were refusing them. Neither the father nor grandmother could give them adequate care and did not have money to buy formula for them. They would try to raise them on cow's milk and corn meal porridge. The results were usually fatal. It is also contrary to their custom to allow them to be adopted. I have had fathers tell me they would rather "put them six feet under" than allow them to be adopted.*

*Often a grief-stricken father would come with his newborn baby wrapped in a rag and ask us to keep his baby for him after the death of the mother. When I was forced to turn one away because of lack of space, I felt as though I were pronouncing a death sentence. We made space in our womens ward to keep up to twelve babies at one time. When they were a year or two old and could survive on the local food, we would return them to their father who had probably remarried by that time. Those precious little babies really stole our hearts. We became so attached to them that it was hard for us to send them home not knowing whether they would be properly cared for or not. Some received good care and some did not. Often one would return to the hospital a few weeks or months later suffering from malnutrition and starvation. Some even died in my arms.*

*These children we raised became very special to us. Petie's mother, a little fourteen-year-old girl, died by the roadside as she was walking to the hospital for delivery. When the family saw she was not going to make it in time for delivery, they sent a runner ahead for us to come and help her. By the time we arrived she had delivered a boy named Petie. He was very much alive, though she was dead. We raised him in the hospital and loved him very much.*

*Another father brought his twin sons to us with a very sad story. The mother developed a postpartum psychosis after delivery and wanted to destroy the babies. Her next-door neighbor saw her throwing one of the babies on the ground, trying to kill it. She rushed over and rescued the baby from her. She found Leo, the other twin, in a pot of water where the distraught mother was attempting to kill him. Of course we made room for them. It seemed the sadder the background, the more we loved the babies.*

*Then there was Belia, whose father and schoolgirl mother were very distantly related. In cases like this, the mother and father are forgiven, but the baby is seen as "no good" and should not be allowed to live. These babies, called "no good," were starved until they became very weak. How we learned to love these little unloved babies.*

*The highlights of my work in Kenya were the well baby clinics, family planning clinics, and the little orphans.*

## Chapter 45

# Bible Translation Committee

$A$bout seventeen different tribal languages were spoken in North Kavirondo, all of similar origin. With the exception of the Psalms, Proverbs, and many Old Testament stories, none of the Old Testament was yet available to the people except in English and Swahili Bibles.

The American, British, and foreign Bible societies tried to work together with the education department to combine the seventeen different dialects into one language called the Luyia. It would be more economical to print larger quantities of the one language than to put the Bible into so many different dialects. Then, too, the spelling had become a problem in the schools. The time had come for a unified spelling of the languages. Many of the root stems were similar, but the prefixes differed slightly. Of course, some words had different meanings, but education would change these meanings unless they were entirely opposite. Many of the variables caused a great deal of resistance and controversies on the part of those whose words were changed.

A Bible translation committee was formed. Bishop Leonard Beecher, then the archbishop of the Anglican Church of East

Africa, became the chairperson of the committee. Lee Appleby from the Church Missionary Society was the secretary and the chief translator. Each mission was invited to send a missionary representative as well as African representatives from as many tribes as possible to attend the meetings. In between committee meetings, Lee Appleby worked with a group of Africans to prepare the script for the committee to discuss. The Church of God represented four tribes: Bunyore, Kakamega, Kisa, and Butsoso. These tribes all used the Olunyore New Testament, so they would most likely accept the change with no great controversy.

Mabel Baker, our senior missionary, with her experience and linguistic expertise, represented our mission. After sitting through the long sessions that usually lasted for several days, no one could ever again fail to appreciate translators of the Bible. One sensed the carefulness and responsibility they all felt as they attempted to make the Word of God clear. Yet in a language such as the one we were dealing with, many of the terms were untranslatable. How could they understand snow? A suitable substitution had to be made to convey meaning to them. Snow is unknown on the equator, at least in the local community. But as people leave home and become more knowledgeable, the translation may need to be changed. Swahili words are rapidly replacing other less-known words, used only by the older people of the tribe. The translator needs to adjust to the understanding of the people.

After spending several sessions trying to find a phrase equivalent to "Abraham falling on his face before the Lord," the secretary reread the script a final time before submitting it to the British and Foreign Bible Society. One young African exclaimed, "I don't think Abraham could do that at ninety years of age."

"What did we say he did?" she asked.

"I can't tell you but I will show you. It may take more room than you have here," he uttered as he began pushing the chairs aside.

Then he turned a cartwheel before the class. Of course, the committee felt foolish, but how little the Word of God would have portrayed in that nonsensical message had it gone through without detection. The committee deleted the phrase and proceeded to search for a better one.

Another problem arose concerning the word *okhulama*. It meant "to pray" in one particular area. All of the C.M.S. hymnals were printed with *Lama*. But in our area the same word meant "to curse."

Eventually, after about twenty years, the entire Bible was translated and printed in the Luyia language. A great dedication and celebration was held at the Kima church the day the first copies were sold. It was indeed a great day for all the seventeen tribes who now have access to their first edition of a complete Bible in an understandable language. To some, the language may seem a bit strange, but in a few years they will accept it as all new things are accepted and will never think about it again. Young people will grow up using the new language, both in school and in church.

Grace Donohew became the official translator on the Kima mission after Mabel Baker retired. She was greatly gifted in languages; she knew and spoke several. After her retirement, she returned to the university and received an advanced degree in one of the African languages.

Grace was also a talented musician. Because of the African's ability to sing, she saw the need of giving them notes to follow in their singing. She printed and translated *Waves of Devotion* into the Luyia language and tediously added the notes to the words.

The old printing press, now obsolete, is no longer used. Douglas Welch, with African workers, began printing at the Mwihila Mission with more modern equipment.

The translation work began with a very limited and small beginning, but it brought to the people one of the greatest blessings they could ever hope to have—the written Word of God. Not only the Word, but with it came the ability and training to learn to read it.

From the earliest days on, all the new Christians entered a baptismal class for a year. It was called the reader's class. Here the readers acquired as much teaching as they could from the Bible. They were supposed to learn to read, too, for the Bible was the Christian's strength.

A number of years ago, a new shipment of the New Testament with the Psalms arrived. I happened to be selling the new copies in the bookstore. One of the mission workers came in, untied from a ragged piece of cloth three shillings, which represented a week's work, and asked for a Testament. I said to him, "Harun, do you read?"

"Oh no, I can't read, but I want a copy of the Bible to have in my home. When a guest comes, I'll ask him to read it to me. It's such good food."

As he walked away smiling, he tightly clutched the New Testament to him. How I wished Mabel Baker could have seen him and heard his testimony. She would have said as her father said many years before, "The trip's been paid for."

When a shipment of New Testaments arrives, they are sold quickly, for it could be several years before the next printing would be made in their language.

# Chapter 46

# Mabel Baker Retires

In the year 1953 Mabel Baker had been in Kenya for thirty-nine years. She had come to the Kima Mission with her father via the long route from Johannesburg, South Africa. But when she arrived on the train to Port Florence (later known as Kisumu), she was not met by car, but by four porters with a carrying chair on which she would be carried on her first trip to Kima, while her father rode by her side on a borrowed bicycle.

How different the country must have looked to her after living in the larger cities of South Africa with all the conveniences. Her father had often spoken to the family about Kenya Colony, but this was his first time there. He began the mission in 1905 when he sent Robert Wilson and a number of other missionaries to help him. He loved missions and was responsible for beginning some forty or more missions among the mining camps in South Africa. He loved the Zulus and was interested in seeing them won to Christ.

Although I was one of Mabel's best friends, she seldom spoke of her childhood. Her mother died when she was seven and her father remarried. In 1912, the family went to England to visit the mother's family and Mabel attended a missionary training school prior to coming to Kenya in 1914. She was British but belonged to a family who had lived for several generations in the Union of South Africa. Her father was a practicing lawyer until he became a missionary. His main concern was that of bringing the Word of God to the unreached

Africans. As his daughter, Alberta, said, "He loved to defend a Zulu."

He was a very warm-hearted, generous person. Mabel patterned after him. She was quiet, gentle, always thoughtful of others, wise, trustworthy, dependable, could keep counsel, and was never forward.

Her retirement day was a great opportunity for the Africans to really show their appreciation for her after all the years she had served them. They were not happy that she was leaving them, for they had wanted to bury her in their own soil with their own hands, and now that special privilege would not be theirs. One of the toastmasters said, "Her body will go to South Africa, but her heart will remain with us in Kenya."

Feasts among the Africans became a frequent occasion during her last few weeks with them. No expense was too great to show their love for her. Elaborate cakes were found on many of the tables of the homes in which she was an honored guest. The African church had a large farewell service in which they told her in two languages how much they had appreciated her and her work.

In order to insure her the comforts of her last days, they purchased a beautifully made dresser, a bookcase, a chieftain's stool, and a lounge chair all made of *mvuli*, an African wood. The Sunday schools gave her money to purchase books.

She was our dearest friend. From her lips we had received our first Olunyore lesson; her feet guided some of us over the hills and through the valleys to churches, schools, the home of some ill one, or perhaps to lay a bunch of flowers on the grave of a friend who had passed on. She never forgot the niceties of life and was always conscious of people's sorrows or troubles. With just a word of encouragement, a handshake, and extending her sympathy, she lifted many a heart. Her words changed a difficult problem into one of understanding and helpfulness. One of the Africans' tributes was that they could never bring any gossip to her, for she would always reply that they should pray and try to help the offender.

As she left, the linguistic tongue and the knowledge of the Olunyore language, acquired during thirty-nine years of research, went with her. All of the younger Africans declared that she had a greater Olunyore vocabulary than any of them had. Into their language she translated many of their books, a large portion of Scripture, and, before she left, the New Testament had been revised with the addition of the Psalms. It would require years for anyone to know the language well enough to replace her. Recognition has been given by many leading linguists for the excellency of her translation work. The last night on the mission was spent in transferring her accumulation of words into a notebook to be used by her successor. She loved the Olunyore language as a mother loved a child, and through this means she was able to get into the hearts of the people.

Children as well as the younger ministers call her mama, for she had been there as long as they could remember.

Being a youthful person, she seemed surprised one day when retirement time came. Although she was the same age as my mother, I always thought of her as a young person. She could out-walk any of us. And although she never tried to out-talk us, she certainly could do so in her beloved Olunyore.

She was always ready to be accommodating. One day when Margaret LaFont was trying so hard to study Olunyore, she kept being interrupted by the students from the girls school. Mabel said, "Margaret, let us try to get away for a few weeks together so that you can get the foundation of this language." Then she arranged with a friend from another mission to borrow one of the vacant houses on their mission, and she and Margaret went into seclusion for two weeks while they studied the language.

One of the rich experiences I shared with Mabel was during our visits with her very dear friends, Miss Dorthea Boldt and the Herbert Innises. Miss Boldt came to Kenya from South Africa just after the Robert Wilsons began our Kima Mission in 1905. They formed a part of the early development of the 1905-06 mission area in the Kisumu area.

Miss Boldt arrived from South Africa in 1906 and settled at Ogada as an independent missionary. Shortly afterward, she was joined by her very dear friends, the Innises, also from South Africa. They worked with her, helping to get the work established as the Independent Nilotic Mission.

After their first furlough, the Innises went to Nyakatch where they established the African Inland Mission among another group of Luo-speaking Africans.

These people were lifelong friends of Mabel who visited each other regularly through the years. It was a beautiful friendship. On one occasion I remember Mabel telling how she and Miss Boldt crossed the long, hot Kano plain—a distance of about sixty miles from Ogada. Mabel rode her bicycle and Miss Boldt, her donkey—a great price to pay for a rest away from a busy, bustling mission.

The Innises at that time traveled by oxcart when they went to Kisumu to do their shopping. Shopping trips in that day were few and far between. Missionaries lived off the land and maintained their tables by simple living and ingenious culinary planning.

Through the years Mabel nurtured and cherished this very precious friendship with these gracious people, and it was reciprocated. They were always young at heart, full of fun, and always found something to laugh about. After they retired, Miss Boldt and the Innises moved to Kericho where they built a house together with separate apartments but one common living room. One of the cherished moments was the daily tea served punctually at four o'clock. No matter how lowly the biscuits were, they always became elegant when spread with butter and jam. Mabel Baker's ginger snaps still fill my taste buds with a sweet, tangy savor.

Mabel retired in South Africa 1953, but our friendship never wavered. She returned to Kima on three occasions—for the fiftieth anniversary of the mission at Kima, for the dedication of the Baker Elementary School, and once to stay with Lydia and me.

Then I went to visit her in Johannesburg not too long after her retirement. She had a brief time of adjusting from the simple country life of the mission field to the modern hustle and bustle of Johannesburg with its culture and Apartheid. Sensing her culture shock, I suggested that she and I would audit a class in comparative Bantu studies under a renowned teacher at a university in Johannesburg. She asked his permission and he seemed eager to have us come to add another to the vast variety of over one thousand Bantu languages.

He was very cordial and interested in our language, Olunyore. I often referred in class to Mabel's language ability and her expertise of many years. She was persuaded to join the class and it soon bridged the gap between the two cultures. She had a contribution to make to the class and enjoyed it immensely for the term.

Finally at the age of 92, Mabel passed away with a brief stroke that took her home easily. I lost the best friend I had ever had. She was a great woman who followed all the principles of Christianity as Jesus taught them.

## Chapter 47

# Carl and Eva-Clare Kardatzke

In 1953, Carl and Eva-Clare Kardatzke and their three children, Howard, Phyllis, and Lois, came to Kenya for one year on a Fulbright Scholarship. While there, Carl was instrumental in getting the African Inland Mission School at Kijabe accredited. This is where the children of the missionaries attended school. The Kardatzke children attended the school during the Mau Mau unrest, and Howard took his post near the forest during the night of a very severe attack on one of the nearby African villages.

When the Kardatzkes visited us, the children became excellent missionary workers. Going from house to house with his tool box, Howard put right so many of the neglected jobs that had never been finished or that needed care on the mission. We had no indoor plumbing then. Before the Kardatzkes left, the problem had been taken care of. New ceilings replaced the old mat ones that dropped occasional lizards our way.

Carl made friends with an Asian electrician in Kisumu and worked with him long enough to learn the rudiments of the trade, and then proceeded to wire our houses. He kept busy. On one of his trips to Kenya he took over the responsibility of the grant-aided schools and supervised them when Cal Brallier went on furlough.

Eva-Clare, or Tip as she is better known, was not idle. During the time we were going to Kisii, she took over the bookstore in my absence and did an excellent job of it. She also worked in the villages with us when we went for women's classes.

One day when she was working at the bookstore, an elderly man came in and asked for a pair of glasses so that he could read. After trying on some old glasses that magnified the print, he was disappointed because he still could not read. The fact was that he had never learned to read, and he had the idea that the glasses held some magic power.

Tip enjoyed the village services and the African choruses. Her big beautiful smile and gracious manner were so much a part of her that, even without their language, she drew everyone to her. Then one day Tip must have picked up a virus or an insect bite, and she had to be taken to the hospital in Kisumu with an extremely high temperature. Her life was held in the balance for several days, but God brought her back again to us.

Carl and Tip were unable to attend their first daughter's wedding while they were in Kenya. In lieu of attending, they talked to Mary Lee on the telephone on her wedding day. That night the missionaries gathered around the family and had a mock wedding that seemed to help the family spirits and kept up their morale.

While they were attempting to keep up their spirits in Kenya, ten thousand miles from their homeland, Cal and Martha Brallier went as envoys to Mary Lee's wedding to represent the missionary family. One of the amusing experiences Cal told about the wedding was that when the best man tried to wear his boutonniere, he found his coat lapel without a boutonniere opening. One helpful soul came with a knife and proceeded to open it just as someone snapped a picture that resembled a stabbing. Carl would have enjoyed that.

On one occasion Tip had gone with us to Kisii. One of our neighbors by the name of Little John had just become a Christian and had brought his fetishes and charms to the church to be destroyed. Usually this occurs outside the church and is a testimony that the man or woman is leaving his or her heathen practices and wants to serve the Lord. It was a rainy night and since it was impossible to make a fire outside, they suggested that he bring the articles into the church and burn them there before the altar. Tip was seated with us on the front row when the bonfire was lit and Little John began to throw his fetishes into it. Suddenly his bag of strong tobacco ignited and the aroma arose like an incense, choking all of us. Tip choked and coughed and managed to utter the words between coughs and tears, "That's the biggest five-cent cigar I have ever smelled."

On their second trip to Kenya in 1955, Carl brought several of the old-fashioned wall phones with the crank handles (not yet declared antiques) with him and installed them on the mission. What a help they were, especially when used between the hospital and the nurses' home to relate the patient's condition. They saved many steps.

The Kardatzke family was certainly like a tonic to the tired missionaries. One night we were called out of our homes to view two men carrying placards that read "Forgotten Fathers." There stood Frank and Carl thinking it was Father's Day and that no one had mentioned it to them. The joke was on them, for in the absence of commercial advertising, they had the wrong day. It was a week too early. Most likely the missionary family was sure to pay the proper honor to those poor rejected souls.

The greatest recreation and about the only one on the mission was playing Rook. We came together once in a while just to relax and have fun. And that we did. It was as much fun to lose as it was to win. Frank LaFont never wanted to stop, especially when he was losing. He would always come up with, "Oh, just one more game. This will be the grand championship," and when he didn't win that game, he would say, "Let's make it the Barb Wire Bath Tub."

When David Gaulke came, we initiated him to our nonsensical playing. But it took him a long time to adjust to it. He was a surgeon and an exacting one, so he played Rook with the same efficiency with which he operated. We all shied away from being his partner, especially Elsie, his wife.

While still speaking of Rook, I must relate a very naughty thing the nurses did when Lowry Quinn, executive secretary of the Missionary Board, came to the mission. He knew that all of us liked to play Rook, and so he challenged three or four of us single girls to a game. He told us he could play as long as we could. He said, "I could play Rook all night." So the game started and all of us were having a great deal of fun. We usually served simple refreshments such as popcorn and orange juice. Time passed and some of us had work to do the next morning, so one of the nurses dropped a phenobarbital tablet in Lowry's orange juice. After a while his eyelids became heavy and he had to give up, with much apology, because he was unable to outplay us. We never did tell him about it.

Years later, the guilty nurse and I were relating the experience when whom should we meet but the late Lowry Quinn's daughter. Trying to clear a guilty conscience or to share the joke, we told her of the experience. She thoroughly enjoyed it, for she said he never wanted to stop playing Rook. Like Frank LaFont, he always said, "Just one more game."

# Chapter 48

# The Need for Theological Training

Ever since the mission began, Bible teaching was one of the strongest emphases on the mission stations. Regular Bible classes were conducted in all of the class rooms, both in the villages and on the mission. The baptismal classes presented the concepts of Christian living. Most of the missionaries stressed it through their various departments. Several set aside time to meet with different village groups in regular teaching sessions. Ruben Schwieger, Frank LaFont, Wick Donohew, Jewell Hall, and James Yutzy all contributed to teaching programs with the pastors, while Nora Schwieger, Irene Engst, and I went to the villages with weekly Bible classes for the women. Yet the pastors needed more help. They needed the daily study of the Bible under teachers who were specifically trained to give a systematized course and follow the regular syllabus for training pastors.

In 1953, A. F. Gray came to the mission for that purpose. He and Wick Donohew worked together in establishing the first Bible school at the Kima Mission. It was opened in 1954 with twelve students. The students had very little knowledge of the Old Testament. They had the New Testament and Psalms in their own language but were very eager to learn more about the Old Testament.

Most of them lived in the dormitory and were married men whose homes were within twenty miles of the mission. They returned home to their churches and families on Friday evenings and returned again to school on Sunday evening.

Their fees for the year amounted to about three hundred shillings, or forty-five dollars. That may seem like a small amount to the American people, but most of their yearly incomes do not exceed that amount. The people had to grow most of their food on their small plots of land or they could not survive. The African church helped the pastors to pay their fees, for they would not be able to do it themselves. Out of that amount, the mission furnished them two khaki uniforms, their food, and bedding. A small garden plot was set aside for them to grow a few of their vegetables on the mission compound.

Jairo Asila, Wick and Grace Donohew, and other missionaries became the teaching staff of the new school.

Wick Donohew had many years of experience as a very successful pastor. In 1946 he and Grace went to Germany to give assistance to the war-torn churches there. He often told us the heart-rending stories of the suffering of the people of Europe due to lack of food and homes. Being a strong nation, the German people soon rebuilt their churches and their Bible school. As the Donohews traveled through Europe, they were able to give courage and strength to the many families who now were stronger Christians than ever before.

Being a talented linguist, Grace learned the German language and became one of the interpreters at the World Convention when it met there a number of years ago.

Wick Donohew was a real pastor. His work with the young men in the new Bible school in Kenya made him a pastor to pastors. He was badly afflicted with arthritis and seldom moved a step without pain, but he never lost his sense of Irish wit and humor, which always put him in good stead during some of the difficult problems he had to solve as chairperson of the African Assembly of the Church of God and secretary of the mission. He was pastor to all of the members of the mission staff. There was never a problem we could not talk over with him and come away feeling better for sharing it with him. His kindness and gentleness put him in the good graces of everyone. The children loved to nuzzle up close to him, for he usually carried peppermint candy in his pocket and was willing to share.

The richness of his past experience and how he bore his physical condition were certainly exemplary to the young ministers just beginning their work. Patience and understanding were a part of his daily living.

His wife, Grace, was a gifted teacher, too. She grasped their language quickly as she had done in Europe and, through this media, was able to make an unusual contribution to the Bible school.

Jairo Asila was a great asset to the newly formed Bible school, for he could give excellent guidance in national customs and background. The first class lasted for three years.

With many of the young men advancing in English and the colony now moving toward its independence, it was imperative for the entrance requirements to be upgraded.

The Bible school continued under the Donohews until 1957, when Lew and Wanda Goodrick came to take Wick Donohew's place as secretary of the mission and to assume the principalship of the Bible school. Both these young people were gifted and talented teachers. Wanda was a good musician who continued the work Grace Donohew had begun. Lew had a background of farming and was prepared to teach agriculture that would enhance the farming methods and raise the living standards in their villages.

They had not been in Kenya very long before an epidemic of polio struck again, bringing several of the African children into the hospital. Three-year-old Louella Goodrick was brought to the mission nurse with a high temperature. Thinking it was the ever-present malaria, she was given therapy, but the next morning her legs were paralyzed. The doctor diagnosed it as polio. The paralysis was bad, but I remember little Louella saying, "I can wiggle one toe." That gave us all courage.

However, after a short time, the doctor said that they should go home for therapy. Lew was torn between his work and his family. But the staff insisted that the family return to the United States for medical care. In the meantime, Paula, the second daughter, came down with rheumatic fever and she, too, needed special care. The mother could never have traveled alone with two sick children. None of us could understand why such afflictions should come on people who were so badly needed and so dedicated, but God knew, and who were we to question him?

After treatment and therapy, they returned again to Kenya to resume their work. Louella was fitted with braces and crutches and was beginning to learn to handle them very well. Her father built a small swimming pool near the house for the therapy her parents gave her so faithfully.

Lew resumed his role as principal of the Bible school. He was most energetic, not only in his teaching, but also in his outlook for the Africans. He always hoped they would be able to have a better livelihood as a result of what they learned in the school. The St. Joseph, Michigan, church gave a grant of money to begin a tannery in which several Africans were trained in the trade of leatherwork. They turned out many fine specimens of lovely work on a high professional level.

The school continued and the standards were raised. After a while it received the status of the theological college and the entrance requirements included English. Lew worked at the college with great enthusiasm. Wanda was right beside him. Time to them was valuable and was never wasted.

They returned to Kenya after their furlough. Their greatest burden was the healing of Louella, and they continued praying for it until they left the mission in 1966.

Having lived in Florida, not too far from the Goodricks, I never lost complete contact with them, even though we did not get to see each other often. Louella graduated from high school, and as the honor student she had the privilege of leading the procession of the high school at graduation time. She was always a happy, buoyant person; she had made a place for herself. Then she continued school and received her bachelors and masters degrees at the university, driving her own car.

They were a fine family. They loved the Africans and were loved by them.

# Part Four:
# African Church Reaches Out in Missions

## Chapter 49

# Kisii Begins

The church's first contact with the Kisii area in southwestern Kenya was as early as 1944. Obed Kutera and his family moved to Kisii sometime before that to obtain more land in the Kisii area.

Obed was a very congenial person and soon drew the people about him because of his winsome personality and his Christian witness. They loved to sit around the table with the family as he read the Bible and shared with them. While he had not been a pastor, he was a faithful Christian.

They watched him carefully and then one of them finally said, "We like what you are telling us. Can't we start a church?" He not only encouraged them, but helped them build a mud and wattle church in which to worship.

The African Assembly gave him an allowance and later a bicycle for transportation to and from the churches that were beginning to develop in different villages. In 1950, thirteen small churches had been started.

That year, a revival was being held at Obed's home church, the Waluka church at Bunyore. He invited six of the Kisii Christians to accompany him there on the sixty-mile trip.

The meeting was most unusual. The Kisii had never seen or heard anything like it before. There were visitations into the community inviting all the people to come to the meetings.

Prayers were ascending for the souls of the unsaved. People were being saved, people were reconciled, and many came to the altar of prayer to ask forgiveness. They sensed the presence of God among them.

Then one of the Kisii children became very ill. The mother began wailing, "What will I do if my child dies here in a strange country?"

The elders put their hands on her and said, "Don't fret, God is here. He can heal your child." They prayed and soon the child recovered. From that moment on, the revival burned deeply into the hearts of all present, and the Spirit of God led many more of the leaders to the altar.

All during the meeting, the Kisii people watched and listened as they gained new insights into what Christianity was, for they were beginners in the faith. During one of the services, a little old Masai woman, a converted witch doctor from the Kisii area, stood up and said to the church people, "You Bunyore people have everything. You have good churches, good homes, schools, and God. Your God even heals your bodies. We Kisii have nothing. You are like people who have eaten all the meat from a strong, healthy cow, and now you are still gnawing on the bones. Can't you send us a little bone so that we can know God, too?"

The feeling was tense in the congregation that day, and the Spirit of God was manifested in the urgency that seemed to pass from person to person.

Finally one of the elders stood up and said, "We must do something about this request. Let's see if we can raise enough money to send some of our people down there to help these people."

That day the Bunyore church became a missionary church. They raised enough money to hire a bus and take about thirty people one hundred miles to Kisii to witness to them. When we learned that they were going, Mabel Baker, Lydia Hansen and I, and some African elders decided to go with them.

As we drew near we noticed that the church had just been built. The mud on the walls was scarcely dry, and the door and windows were merely holes in the wall. It was packed and the Bunyore guests were sitting on the newly made mud platform. They had improvised pews by pounding forked sticks into the dirt floor; the sticks braced the wooden poles used for pews, and they were all filled with people. They had improvised an altar at the front of the church.

Toward the end of the service, four women came forward to pray. Daudi Otieno turned to the three of us and asked us to pray with them. We didn't know their language and we each had to use an interpreter. I spoke in Luyia and Miriam, Obed's wife, interpreted for me in Gusii. Finally, after attempting to explain the way of salvation to one woman, I said, "Now will you pray and ask God to save you?"

"Pray? What is prayer?" she asked. Then I realized how futile our efforts had been. They had asked for a bone and that was all we were able to give them.

The next day, we went to the present mission site at Obedo. Mabel Baker spoke, the altar call was given again, and about forty people knelt for prayer. We did not know how to help them with all their problems. They were such that could be changed only by God.

We left with heavy hearts. Truly the Lord was speaking to all of us. These people needed God so badly. It was impossible to dismiss the burden of the four women who knelt at the altar. We were unable to meet their needs because of our lack of proper communication. Their only hope was their own trained people. Missionaries were needed to help train their people in methods of leadership and instruction in the Bible. These people needed schools to become literate and more self-reliant. They were not turning their backs on Christianity, but welcomed it, and desired it. They had to know the Christian concepts if they were to win others to Christ.

The churches that had been started were handicapped because they lacked leadership. The preachers could only preach what they had heard, for at that time most could scarcely read.

Through Obed's witness and with the help of the young Kisii believers, their enthusiasm spread into the surrounding areas. This spark ignited and changed the hearts of the African people into Christians. Witch doctors would accept the message and throw witchcraft paraphernalia into the fire.

One of the most encouraging features was the fact that the congregations consisted mostly of young people. Obed and his helpers had begun nine different churches within a radius of forty miles. The assembly finally gave him a bicycle to reach the outlying areas. With the elders, he traveled to and visited all the churches in order to nurture them.

Several missionaries went to Kisii to preach and to encourage the people. In February 1954 Adam Miller, president of the Missionary Board, wrote very encouragingly about Kisii. At this time, the main mission thrust was to establish the Mwihila Hospital that had been on the drawing board for years. Funds and personnel were unavailable. The best we could do was to go once a month, hold a dispensary with them, and try to visit the churches on Sundays. Nothing permanent could be done until it had been approved as a mission with the land surveyed by the government. Whether the Missionary Board was willing to assume a new mission station was now the greatest problem. "Would it snowball and demand similar growth as Mwihila and Kima had done?" was the Board's question. With the dispensary available, would there be a demand for a hospital?

Then a group of Kisii elders with Pastor Obed came to us and asked Lydia Hansen and me to come there as missionaries. We both had our responsibilities as full-time missionaries, but there was little to hinder us from going down once a month if that would satisfy them. When we went, Lydia and I had a dispensary on Saturday. That only increased our burden, for the first day a long line of ninety people stood all day long until they could get treatment. Some of the people were very ill. There was no question of need; it was everywhere.

How kind and hospitable Obed and Miriam were to us. They gave us their home for the night, fed us, and treated us like royalty in their home. Obed was a happy person and had winsome ways. He loved to laugh and joke with the people. Miriam was an excellent hostess. During 1953, we made four trips to Kisii and spent several days on each visit.

The mission staff gave unanimous approval for us to go. For several years we had been inconveniencing Obed and Miriam by using their home for our living quarters. The staff voted unanimously to build a safari house for Lydia and me at Kisii.

When final arrangements were made, the staff gave us two weeks a month to work at Kisii, with the understanding that we dare not neglect our work at Kima. The Africans came to our rescue and began to assume the work we had been doing. Rita Ayanga took over the nearby Bible classes and the missionary societies, and did an excellent job. Elder Enoch Olando had a bicycle and he taught the far-away Bible classes that Rita could not walk to. Ruth Kilmer, missionary from Egypt for one year, helped with the sewing groups, and Eva-Clare Kardatzke helped in the bookstore during the year she was in Kenya.

The womens missionary societies had seen and felt the needs of the Kisii when they were there for a service. The women of Bunyore gave money for windows and doors for the church, school, and building complex used for a dispensary.

A young Bunyore couple came down to be our first head master and teacher at Ibeno. We had a fine Kisii teacher there, too, who worked with George Kutwa and his wife, Rosemary. Until the government separated the school and church plots, the building was an all-purpose building.

Now we were able to begin regular Bible classes with the pastors. About nine or ten attended regularly. For one week each month they attended classes from Monday evening until Friday morning, returning then to their churches for the weekend. Lydia also took care of the ill ones in the temporary dispensary. Some of the men had traveled a long way. One man walked forty miles to attend the class. I asked him how long it usually took him to come to class, and he said, "Well, if I keep walking and do not stop, I can leave home at seven o'clock in the morning and get here by four in the afternoon." They never missed a session.

Moving the dispensary equipment to and from Kima each time became a burden. Also, we needed a place for our class when the rains began. So that was to be the next urgent project. We discussed it with the womens organizations. They pledged and gave us two thousand shillings to finish the dispensary and classroom. The Kisii people built a mud and wattle hut for the dispensary.

Perhaps the greatest advantage of the new Kisii mission was the outlet it gave for the Church of God in Bunyore to cross into another culture with the gospel. We asked for help from the Bunyore church and they marvelously contributed toward its growth, both in finances and leadership.

John Owor, a Bunyore businessman who owned a car, came with one of our fine Christian leaders, Micah Olubaya, and brought the president of the Bunyore Womens Missionary Society, Dinah Jonah, and Lois Zaddock with them for revival meetings among the Kisii people. With a number of the Kisii elders, they walked from house to house, witnessing and preaching to the people. They allowed themselves one day only in each village, and the results were over and above all they could have possibly hoped for. At the end of their safari, they reported more than four hundred souls saved.

The Bible school at Kima had sent groups down to witness to the Kisii on different occasions. On one trip, the Kisii elders were especially impressed with Hezron Marisia. They invited him to come and live and work with them. He had been the chaplain in the Bible school at Kima for a number of years, and so he and his wife, Margaret, prayed about it, and the womens missionary societies assumed his support for a year. A very successful womens convention was held at Kisii.

### David and Elsie Gaulke Help at Ibeno

David and Elsie Gaulke served in Kenya from 1953-58 after

they were forced to leave their work in West China during the revolution. To say they were heartbroken is putting it mildly; all their hopes for a lifework in China had been dissolved. The years of language study seemed wasted. The time spent in scrubbing the old temple to be used as a hospital was now history. They were burdened greatly about the hospital in China left in the hands of new Christians.

After a brief time in Kenya in 1949, the Gaulkes went to the United States, then returned in 1953 to build the hospital at Mwihila.

At this time, we were making monthly trips to Kisii. When the medical needs of the Kisii people were presented to the Gaulkes, they offered to help one weekend a month. How eager and enthusiastic Elsie became! She loved Kisii with its hills, its nippy, cool nights, and its people with their great needs.

Our weekends in Kisii were filled with work and happy experiences. No one minds being tired when work is enjoyable, and it was.

Our dispensary was conducted in the school building. The doctor examined patients in one room behind a mat wall, while Elsie and Lydia carried out the orders of the doctor in the second room, which doubled as a church.

Each safari was an adventure before the Gaulkes became overworked with the building and organization of the new hospital at Mwihila. Elsie, too, became heavily involved in the training of the nurses. How they enjoyed visiting the little Kisii churches for services where they always preached and we all remained for a dinner of *obusuma* and chicken.

I registered the patients for the doctor and then translated into Luyia for him. One of the Africans translated again into Gusii. By the time the answers came back to the doctor, I often accused him of taking a nap between questions. How would you like to go through three languages to tell the doctor about your arthritis? Elsie and Lydia did the treatments in the other room.

We usually left home the first Friday of each month, and after traveling in our Jeep for the hundred miles between our two homes, we arrived at our little corrugated metal safari house. After traveling on the red dusty roads, we were so thankful for the water in the rain tank. Lately it had been nearly empty. There was usually enough left at the very bottom to wash the red dust off our faces.

Then we would get the house dusted and the kerosene refrigerator lit and everything ready for the traditional 6:30 A.M.

service. By the time the service had ended, the patients began to come for treatment and had accumulated outside our door in a crowd, hoping to be the first one.

When I was free, I would help Lydia with the records while she examined the patients. They did not trust Lydia, for unless she had a stethoscope and a hypo needle, they did not think she had the power of healing.

On one occasion, Lydia forgot to bring the stethoscope from home, and when one woman found out that she did not have it, she said, "I'll wait for the doctor." On another occasion, when Richard Smith had first come and had finished examining a woman, she proclaimed in a loud voice, "He didn't examine the pain in my knee with that thing."

## First Visit to the Masai

Obed had been speaking of one of the Luyia families who had settled near the Masai border and wanted us to visit their congregation at a place called Suna, near the Tanganyika border. It was about sixty-five miles south of Ibeno, where we have the work among the Kisii people. They had worshiped with another evangelical group but longed for the day when they could be identified with a Church of God congregation. Lydia, Obed, George Kutwa, our school teacher, and I went to Suna on the last Sunday of our two week stay at Kisii. David and Joan Livingston were on the Ibeno mission that weekend, so they agreed to take the Sunday services. Our sixty-five-mile trip began early in the morning since roads were not very good at that time.

Lydia gives an account of our stay in Kisii:

*The people gathered slowly. During the service, Lima spoke in Luyia, the dialect of our part of Kenya. Her talk was understood by the fifty or more Kisa and Bunyore who were present. It was translated again into Swahili for ten or more Masai and was translated again into Luo for the fourteen from the Luo tribe.*

*When the altar call was given, one of the Masai men brought three of the Masai women to the altar. They had been in Sunday school prior to this service and had put the Sunday school papers given them into the lobes of their ears for safe keeping. The Masai was a head man and was now in the baptismal class, so, like Andrew, he brought his friends.*

*The Masai were hard to win. Missionaries have worked with this group of people for years and they have responded in small numbers only. Surely there was a way for the Word of God to reach them. One group of Christians said that the Masai would come to the services, push their spears into the ground in front of them, crouch there until they have heard enough, then get up and walk away. But these at Kisii were staying longer and longer until they had remained for the entire service, and now the first one of them had enrolled in the baptismal class.*

## The Kisii Revival, April 1958

In response to a call from the Kisii churches, four Bunyore Christians went to assist the Kisii missionaries and ministers to conduct a series of revivals in the twelve churches there, as well as to offer their assistance in a youth revival and womens convention at the Ibeno Mission Station.

John Owor reports on the revival:

*Because of lack of time, we had to allow ourselves only one day in each village. The general pattern was to hold a service at 11:00 A.M. and another at 2:00 P.M., followed by visitation in the community. Each person contacted was invited to attend the revival the next morning at 7:00 A.M. Sometimes we visited until dark.*

*As soon as the early morning service was over and we had worked with the people at the altar, we ate quickly and hurried on to the next village.*

*Micah Obbubayi, John Owor, Obed Kutera, Dinah Johanah and Lois Zaddock, together with some of the Kisii ministers, spent long hours walking up and down the hills with a burning testimony to the people. They all took turns preaching, testifying, or giving valuable assistance at the altar. Whenever time permitted, Lydia Hansen and Lima Lehmer joined them.*

*This revival strengthened the Kisii ministers. The two Bible women in the visiting group lived in the homes of the Kisii women and challenged them to higher standards of living, as well as inspired them spiritually.*

*In one village, eighty-nine came to the Lord. But the big problem lies in nurturing those who return to unchristian homes. Those who can remain close to the church and get their strength from other Christians will remain faithful, but without Christian nurturing, many of those will be lost.*

## New Teachers and a New Church

There is always an advantage in spending a number of years in a certain place, for the dividends are tremendous. We were dependent on the Bunyore people for assistance in beginning the work at Kisii. Many years before, two little boys, still preschool age, attended the nursery school. When they grew up, they attended the teacher training center at Mwihila, married, and became teachers. We invited them to come to Kisii to help us. One of their parents said, "Of course, you should go; Miss Lehmer is your mother." Of these two young men and their wives one family went to Nyataro and the other to Mobomba. The Nyataro people took care of the building of their school, but the other area was not progressive. It took a long time to get the school under way.

Lydia Hansen and Phyllis Kardatzke helped the people carry the grass from the swamp in order to keep the people encouraged long enough to thatch the building. We sat there day after day until it was finished. They had been holding school in one of the rooms and had made very crude desks and seats by pounding poles into the ground and nailing boards to the top of them. The government promised us a school in that area if we could have two classrooms, with thirty pupils each, and a teacher's house. There were no funds and the people had little money and less enthusiasm. We examined the one classroom with the improvised desks and seats. Abraham Lincoln learned with that sort of an arrangement. Who knows, maybe we'd get a president out of this classroom. We took Kimwa, the carpenter who helped us at the mission, with us and he soon had sawed up a few logs and pounded them into the hard soil. A carpenter shop down over the hill had a few wide boards just the right size, so Lydia and I put our coins together and purchased them. With a few spikes, even President Abe would have been happy to learn his letters there. The teacher's house still had no doors or windows. The school was soon approved.

The teachers' wives were teachers also, but they soon became involved with the women of the church who asked them to begin the women's missionary societies and teach them to sew. Through this adventure, the wives became a part of the church community. Surely God was good to us, in the way he always sent the help we needed.

A number of years later, when my husband and I returned to Ibeno for a visit, I suggested that we go up the hill to see the Mobamba school. It had grown and covered the entire hillside. The headmaster told us that he had over six-hundred children enrolled and one-hundred forty in the first grade.

One of the new areas requested us to come and measure a church and school in the Namageso area. The date was set and the headman came with his men to do the official gazetting. The only way through at that time was across a valley with a thickly matted, knee-deep swamp. On our first trip, I said to Obed, "Aren't there snakes in that swamp?" Laughing good-naturedly, he replied, "Oh, we'll just step on them." Lydia had a pair of boots that we shared. The first one across wore the boots, and then our escorts would return them to the remaining person for the second trip.

The meadow leading to the swamp was a beautiful spot and we remember the graceful ballet dance put on for our special benefit by the golden crested crane, the Kenya state bird.

We soon arrived at our destination where a large group had already gathered. This was a great occasion for the village. When we went there the first time, Obed took us to a spot at the top of the hill where we were starting a church. Then he turned us to the left and said, "Look as far as you can see; you will not see a church or school anywhere." We looked over miles and miles of rolling hills. Then again he said, "Now look as far as you can see ahead of you"; the results were the same. The third time, he said, "Now look to your right," and all we could see were hills and more hills as they overlapped. "They need the gospel," he added.

The group waited with anticipation. This would be their first school and they were excited about it. We had already built a church there. At the end of the ceremony, they asked us to come into the temporary building they had already built for a church to eat of the feast they had prepared for the guests. They had killed a sheep for the occasion.

On Easter day, 1959, twenty-six were baptized at the Ibeno church. The next Sunday, forty miles north of us, thirteen more were baptized and received their first communion. The crowd was so large that the windows were packed with children and it was not possible to see the notes to play on the little organ we carried with us. There was a happy spirit among the children as they pushed and shoved to get nearer. Lydia took them outside and gave them a Bible story until the service was finished. They always loved to receive a Sunday school leaflet sent from the Sunday school classes in the United States. Seventy of them wanted to become Christians. Perhaps they did not know exactly the full meaning, and they needed someone to live with them and teach them.

Missionaries were terribly handicapped to meet all of these needs, and their only hope was in training Sunday school teachers and public school teachers, pastors, to better equip them to grasp knowledge.

Before we left, the church gave us a lovely farewell service. We, at last, had the knowledge that the task God chose for us to do was finished. Ibeno was now a full-fledged mission station.

Our home at Kima looked good again. We were happy to return to it. We were looking forward to getting settled in and getting back to the villages and hospital with a full-time program. Our greatest appreciation to those who served so faithfully in supplying for us while we worked at Kisii. Rita Ayanga, Enoch Olando, Ruth Kilmer, Rosa Bollmeyer, Naomi Sweeny, and others.

We came home looking forward to the visit from our very dear friend, Mabel Baker, who was coming to us from South Africa. Life was more normal again. The rushing and getting ready every fortnight, with all of our equipment, clothing, food, and other articles necessary for living a safari life, were past. The people at Kisii had a family they could depend on thirty days each month.

# Chapter 50

# Jane and Samuel Betts

Jane Ryan came to Kenya in 1952 and went to the Ingotse Mission to work at the dispensary. By this time a dispensary had been completed along the road for her to treat the many needy patients.

She speaks for herself as she tells of her first days there:

*As a missionary nurse at the Ingotse Station, I have been kept very busy. The giving of medical aid is a little more difficult at our Ingotse station than it is at our main station at Kima because the people are more superstitious. Medicine men or witch doctors are still quite common among the Butsotso tribe among whom we work. Children often wear charms of rocks, hair, skin, or tail of some animal around their necks. It was common practice to cut the part of the body that is hurting to let the pain out, and many come to us with such cuts on their bodies. Sometimes children come with cow dung on their heads. The people thought this has great curative value.*

*Every day we have a worship service for the people we treat at the dispensary. The attendance at these daily meetings ranges from seventy to more than a hundred. We try to help the people spiritually while we are helping them physically. We are not at all satisfied with the extent of this work and we are trying to find better ways of meeting their spiritual needs.*

*Some Bible study classes are being planned for the dispensary patients.*

*A prenatal clinic assists the women, but a place is needed to put these women so that they can rest for a while after their babies come. Because there is no such place, a mother must leave shortly after her baby has been delivered. Recently a mother gave birth to a child at eight o'clock in the morning. She rested until noon and got up and carried her baby home.*

*The women are interested in sewing and are glad to attend the sewing classes. Most of the class time the women make baby quilts. Bible study is also held during the class period. Jane returned home in 1956 and was married to Samuel Betts. Then they returned as full-time missionaries at the Kisii Mission station at Ibeno where they worked for a full term.*

Sam and Jane Betts spent their first year serving in various ways in the older stations—Kima, Ingotse, and Mwihila—and spending much time studying the Gusii language. Then the Bettses went to the newly developed mission station at Ibeno, Kisii.

Successful revivals in the Kisii area have brought success to the fifteen village churches and many are beginning to feel the need of expansion. Youth rallies and revivals are providing the need for good leadership among the young people. Under their leadership three young men went to the Kima Bible School for training. Only eight of the fifteen churches have pastors.

### President Kenyatta Dedicates Ibeno Maternity Ward

Lydia Hansen tells of the maternity ward dedication:

*In 1965-66 the Missionary Board asked if I would go to Kisii and see if I could get the Namweyo Maternity Home finished and functioning. It was setting there idle and unfinished. The project had been started on a self-help basis by the people and local government and needed to be completed.*

*Since Irene Engst was returning from furlough and could take over the womens society work, I could be released and was thankful that she was doing it. The African women were now capable of leading singing, teaching Sunday school classes, speaking in public, and organizing conventions in their villages. They knew their Bibles and were able to help with the altar work. They were good evangelists. Rita Ayanga was an ordained minister and she would be working very closely with Irene. The women were now leaders who served with dignity.*

*While I was waiting for Simon and Mae Robinson, who had replaced the Bettses, to move out of the little safari house at*

*Ibeno into their new one nearby, I took a Swahili course in Nairobi. After that, I moved to Shitoli until the little house at Ibeno was available.*

*I discovered the Oxgam Foundation in Nairobi and visited many of the other agencies I heard about to get money to finish the Maternity Home at Ibeno. A little money was forthcoming and with that, we were able to get the building finished.*

*Mr. Namweyo, the chief to whom I appealed for money, told me to give orders to one of the Indian shops in Kisiitown for the things I needed and the government would pay for them. I drew up plans for cupboards, delivery table, stool, baby bassinets, and two writing desks. I ordered beds, mattresses, pillows, and blankets from Nairobi and material to make sheets and pillowcases.*

*Since it was a self-help program, the president of Kenya, the Honorable Jomo Kenyatta, was willing to come to open the building. Plans had been made for his arrival far in advance. The roads were lined with banana stalks that the chief and his men had planted. The beds had not arrived, so Vera Martin and I pushed the mattresses into place on the floor. When the president entered the building, he said, "Where are the beds?" I explained that the ones I had ordered had not yet come and there was not enough money to buy the amount we needed.*

*"How much money do you need?" he shot at me.*

*Quickly trying to figure it, I replied, "Three thousand shillings," about four hundred dollars in United States currency.*

*When we were having tea that the Robinsons and I had prepared, I was presented with a check for three thousand shillings, signed by President Jomo Kenyatta. We could have used twice that much, but my mind was not alert enough for such sudden action.*

Chapter 51

# Kima Theological College

In 1965, after the death of Mildred Williams, the Missionary Board secretary approached Edgar Williams about the possibility of either going to Kenya to become the principal of the Kima Theological College, or of returning to Jamaica. Edgar left the Missionary Board annual meeting a few days before Anderson Camp Meeting began, in time for us to be married at the Harrisburg, Pennsylvania, church. With his children and grandchildren and with my mother and father, sister and brother, we were married in the church I had attended most of my life, and the church built by Edgar and Mildred.

We were commissioned for Kenya at the Anderson Camp Meeting and left shortly afterward. The Missionary Board had hoped that Edgar could attend the language school in Nairobi for three months, but it was time to begin classes. Edgar, Frank LaFont, Norma Borden, and I were the faculty. Later David Crippen and David and Margaret Montague came to teach at the college. An African instructor would teach Swahili to the upperclass students. We arrived in the midst of the rainy season and promptly got stuck in the mud on the hill to the mission. When the car slid off the road into the ditch, Clair

Shultz, then missionary secretary, hitched the car to the Jeep and pulled it back to the crown of the road with the assistance of the crew from the telephone service, This was to become a regular occurrence when anyone left the mission. We often traveled with two cars and used the buddy system, helping each other up and down that sticky hill.

Edgar Williams describes his first week of school:

*We had ended our first full week of school—it seemed like three, for there was so much to getting it launched. There were eighteen new students, six former and five special students who would leave for their pastoral duties at the end of the term. We bed them, house them, and feed them, for this is their home away from home. Some return to their homes over the weekends, for they are active pastors, but most of them remain on the mission. I have to buy the staples—bedding, tools, books, pencils, paper, notebooks, and so forth. The nearest shopping center is twenty miles away away at Kisumu. I teach Old Testament, church history, Acts, and theology. I buy everything except kitchen produce and manage repairs. Lima teaches ten hours of English to the two classes and two hours of Bible history. Three other missionary teachers and one African teacher complete the staff.*

*I went out today and bought a loaf of bread using the native language, and I got the bread, believe it or not. I can greet them, tell them good-bye, and use a few other expressions, many of the sounds are becoming familiar to me. Lima is my interpreter in dealing with the people at the school.*

*We have a good quartermaster in Reverend Hezron Marisia. He also serves as chaplain for the college and is worth his weight in gold to the college and the principal.*

School began rather smoothly for a new principal unacquainted with the culture. Hezron Marisia was certainly a great help to him. Things began to fall into place. However, Edgar was very much disturbed when he learned from the police who stopped him that he had to drive with a large *L* (learner) on his car to show that he was still a novice at driving after fifty years of safe driving. As soon as he took his test and proved capable, they removed the *L*.

It did not take long until we had a full schedule in the villages and became a part of the training program. We always took a group of students with us and they helped lead the services. They enjoyed getting away from the campus and eating some home-cooked chicken and *obusuma*, which was always the pay for the sermon.

As the students neared graduation, they took the communion service and were taught how to administer it. Many of the people had never had communion in their villages, for it seemed to be held only at the mission stations on Easter after the baptismal service. Then, too, there had been a traditional belief that only the original twelve elders administered communion and baptism. This became an integral part of the school program.

During the time when Louella Goodrick was having therapy for polio, a small swimming pool had been built in the yard. When the students were taught baptism, they each took a turn demonstrating in the swimming pool. The principal wanted them all to leave the school with confidence.

Obtaining firewood had always been a problem on the mission. Many years ago Sidney Rogers planted several hundred eucalyptus trees on the lower part of the mission. Many of the trees had grown to about four feet in girth, and they began harvesting one or more for fuel.

As the deficiencies of their diets came to the foreground, we tried to fortify their foods by introducing foods that were taboo to them. Rabbit was a rodent to them and they did not eat it. Edgar bought a pair and began raising them. The people shrugged their shoulders and said they did not eat them.

We began by inviting the students to our home for formal meals, to introduce them to a different diet than the regular cornmeal mush, and to teach them European table etiquette. One person came back from a large conference in Nairobi to which Bob Pierce invited all the Kenya ministers. They did not know how to handle knives and forks since their food had never been eaten that way, and it became painfully embarrassing for them in attempting to use the unfamiliar cutlery.

So we invited one group who knew the art of eating at a European table, and then we invited a new group to come with them. There was no embarrassment, for it became a class for them and they felt very much at ease as they acquired the knack. Actually we often offended them by picking a piece of chicken up by the bone and eating it. An African child would be punished for not eating properly because he or she would be considered greedy. They kept one hand in their lap and ate with the other.

Then we prepared rabbit and passed it around. Everyone took a share and remarked how delicious the chicken was. We gave them seconds, and then when the meal was finished, we told them that it was not chicken, but rabbit. The next session found them with pride bringing a new group in to enjoy the new food. One of the things for which they thanked us as they left school was teaching them how to eat this way.

The native corn yielded a small crop and much of it was simply nubbins. At that time the agricultural department brought in hybrid corn, and Edgar began buying the hybrid corn and planting it in the school garden. The difference in the yield was beyond their comprehension. All of them wanted him to buy corn for them to use.

Then when we made a trip to Nairobi, we purchased several Rhode Island Red chickens, and raised them. When they began laying eggs, we gave them a setting of eggs. A year later when we went into the villages, we were presented with a large Rhode Island rooster.

They enjoyed the cakes we served them and they wanted to know how they were made. This gave us the opportunity we were looking for, a class for minister's wives. During several vacations we invited the pastors' wives to come in and two of our women school teachers, former students of mine, taught them how to prepare various foods to supplement their diets.

In the villages, we saw a different need than the one we were meeting at the college—that of training for the many self-made pastors. The college men were being trained as leaders and teachers. Some would become executives, and they would not be sent back to the villages, since they were training to replace the missionaries. What could we do as an institution to give them a boost in the villages? The principal talked it over with the board of governors, who were also concerned. Would it be possible to have the pastors come in for classes and then return to their churches over the weekend? Their classes would have to be in Luyia and the lessons would have to be translated into their native tongue, for none of them were far enough advanced to study in English. Yet training would upgrade the village churches.

The proper steps of approval were secured from the local board of governors.

Then the request was sent to the Missionary Board to approve the idea of enrolling a dozen settled pastors for special training in Bible and pastoral methods in the vernacular for one year. After the usual discusion of pros and cons, the board approved and asked for a budget. The budget did not nearly cover the entire program, but we had to launch the program or wait another year to begin it. By the time the money arrived, the students were already in the classroom.

Harley Richardson, a former maintenance missionary at Mwihila Hospital, wrote to us asking for the picture of one of the students for his Sunday school class to support. Instead, Edgar sent a picture of the entire class of the Luyia-speaking students and then forgot about it. At Christmastime, a check came from that Sunday school class with the exact amount to operate the class for the year. This happened for the next two years while we were there. God himself spoke to them, for they did not know how much was needed and we never told them of our needs.

The new pastors class came in and adjusted very well. Edgar thought they would not want to take their share of the work in the garden, but there was no work that they would not attempt to do. As the class was selected, each district had the privilege of choosing the one they felt would best represent their group. All were most cooperative and really appreciated the privilege.

When Edgar was asked to go to the Kima Theological School, it was with the purpose of training an African to assume the office of principal. Byrum Makokha would be returning from the United States with his master's degree to assume this responsibility. The first year he would be assistant principal, the second co-principal, and the last as principal. He then became the executive secretary of the African Assembly, which office he holds to this day. He returned to the States and earned a doctoral degree.

Many changes were taking place on the mission at this time. New boundaries were set for the different institutions with definite demarcation lines. The girls school was set apart from the mission. The public playing field was in the center of the Bible school compound but had to be moved to the far end of the mission to provide space for the new McCoy Memorial Chapel, which would then be in the center of the KTC buildings. Land was greatly limited in this very densely populated area, and there was no possiblity of expansion beyond the mission's borders. The only available space for the playing field was in a grove of more than a hundred-thirty-year-old eucalyptus trees. The trees had to be removed, and the tremendously large boulders, many as large as a house, had to go, too.

Edgar Williams began this nearly impossible task after the board of governors' building plans were drawn up. With a bulldozer, it may have been cleared in a few week's time, but the trees had to removed by their roots, by hand labor digging around the tree base and cutting the tap roots in order to pull out the roots when the tree fell.

Wood was very scarce in the area and the women of the villages would assist in disposing of the limbs and branches by carrying them away for fuel. The larger tree trunks and heavy limbs were sawed and sold to pay for the labor of having them removed.

Then came the rocks. The larger and surface ones were dynamited by a local firm. The money ran out, and still many of the surface granite rocks remained. These had to be removed by building fires over them and burning them to the point that they exploded when water or rain struck them. The rocks were also sold for building purposes. With a space cleared for the field, a great deal of controversy arose from those in the community who had used it for games since the beginning of the mission, as well as from the herd boys who used it for a grazing ground for their cattle.

The master building plan had begun for the Kima Theological College. The first building was the college chapel, which was constructed in the center of the old playing field.

At the end of the first year, six graduated. Three of them went to the International Theological Seminary at Limuru for additional training, and the other three would return for a fourth year of work at the college.

The Kima Theological College became a part of the Kenya Theological Seminary Council and they met periodically in Limuru to discuss this type of education and to share their findings.

The second-year class sent another three graduates to Limuru for further study. Most of these young men continued their studies in the United States. Each year a new Luyia class of twelve pastors came to study for a year and then went back to their villages with training that greatly enhanced the programs of the entire district.

At the end of our term, we had graduated thirty-six one-year pastors who spoke the vernacular and sent them out for ministry in the village churches. The three-year class turned out many of our best leaders. The combining of the two classes formed an enrichment program needed at that time to unite the pastors and young men of the church. There was a time of sharing and understanding between the two groups that developed under those circumstances of living and sharing together.

Regular class programs are carried out now as an extension of the college by faculty members as they take instruction into the villages for the pastoral training.

# Part Five: Independence

## Chapter 52

# Independence for Kenya

Lydia Hansen was present at the Kenyan independence celebration. She relates,

*On December 12, 1963, a shout of joy burst from the throats
of a quarter of a million people in Nairobi, capital of Kenya.
Prince Philip, on behalf of the Queen of England, handed
President Jomo Kenyatta the instruments that symbolized
Kenya's independence.*

*In his speech, the president stressed the need for all Africans,
East Indians, and Europeans alike to live together in the spirit
of Harambee, which means "working together for the common
good," the slogan adopted for the new Kenya. Kenyatta then
waved his fly whisk and called out to the crowd, "Harambee,
Harambee, Harambee." The people answered each time from
every corner of the stadium, "Yeeeeee—ee."*

*Many who had lived under the protection of the British flag
for many years felt a touch of sadness when at midnight,
amidst the playing of the national anthem, the Union Jack
came slowly down. However, cheers and wild clapping of
hands resounded from the bleachers as the green, black, red,
and white striped flag of Kenya, with its shield superimposed*

*in the middle, was run up. It was a day of joy and happiness for them.*

In July, 1969, Tom Mboya, a rising Kenya political and labor leader of some note, was shot down in a drug store in Nairobi. It was a sad occasion, but God overruled it through one of our fine church members. Susie Litondo, wife of our Marikano Center pastor in Nairobi, wanted to pay condolences to the widow. Taking her hymnbook, she started to the Mboya house where his body lay in state.

The government officials wearing uniforms with their lion crested hats stood near his bier. A group of pagan relatives can cause a great deal of pandemonium at a funeral by shrieking, making shrill loud cries, and dancing about the yard. This was only too true there.

Being a Christian, Susie stepped quietly through the mob, walked to the side of the deceased, opened her hymnbook, and began to sing in her beautiful, rich soprano voice. Others came and joined her and the noise quieted down. In a short time, chairs were brought for the group who by this time had formed a choir. The group sang from 10:00 A.M. until 4:00 P.M. Then Susie went to one of the officials and asked permission to go to feed her husband. But instead, he begged her to stay. "You've quieted the mob. Please stay," they told her. She remained a while longer and then left, promising to return.

She ate and asked her husband, Timothy, to accompany her. "Susie, we can't go. The town is too dangerous. Riots, break-ins, and all sorts of quarrels were arising. The entire city is under marshall law. The police are using tear gas."

At her insistence he went, and as he walked to the entrance of the yard, the government officials left their posts of duty, and stretched forth their hand to Timothy with their greeting, *"Milembe Omwibali"* [peace, teacher]. For more than fifty years Timothy Litondo had taught in the primary schools, Kima Boys School, Mwihila Teacher Training Center, and, finally, was one of Cal Brallier's assistant supervisors. These were his students, now people in places of high authority, who had been brought up in the Church of God schools. This is what the early years of Church of God missions did for Kenya. It gave them education combined with a good sense of Christianity to build a strong nation. Kenya has remained firm because of the influence of all the Christian missions who gave their all for the development of Christian African leaders. Thanks be to God for today's Christian president of Kenya, Daniel T. A. Moi.

**Uhura**

Clair Shultz relates the effect of UHURU on mission work in East Africa:

*One of the most important things that happened to help develop the selfhood of the church was UHURU. This meant freedom from being a colony of England and becoming a republic with its own government. Before this happened in 1963, several missionaries had given much thought to helping the church in Kenya become more self-reliant, but some older African leaders did not want this change. For so many years the "kind and helpful" missionaries had been with the mission and everything had gone so well, so why bother to change? Too, the younger national leaders might get some ideas that would be contrary to the long-established policies of the mission and the older pastors were not so sure this would be helpful to the church as a whole. They would rather take much more time. Some effort had been made during the late fifties and Rev. Daudi Otieno, son of one of the late chiefs of Bunyore (the location of our mission) was elected to be chairperson of the pastors assembly. However, the missionaries still carried much of the responsibility. So some effort had been made, but things were not moving very fast. The independence of Kenya and the establishing of the new nation really gave stimulus to getting on with the development of the Kenya church as an African church in its own right.*

*When Retha and I were requested to go to Kenya, Missionary Board secretary Lester Crose asked us to do what we could to help develop the selfhood of the church. We had previously had some experience in this type of thing, in both Trinidad and Jamaica. Obviously then, we had this in mind when we went to Kenya. So when Kenya received its independence in 1963, things as a whole began to change very rapidly to bring about African leadership in the country. Kenya leaders made up the House of Parliament. In other government positions, such as customs and immigration, black people took office. In the banks, black people were soon to be seen taking places of leadership that used to be held by British or East Indian people. Black leadership was to be noted in many places and they took various types of important responsibility. However, within the church, it was a different story. Missionaries were still holding most of the important positions and it became an embarrassment to us when a government official visited our large church assembly and found white leaders still carrying much of the responsibility. So, as the country as a whole began* to follow Kenyan leadership, it became necessary to spark the church to follow suit.

The big push for church development with its own responsibility started shortly after Kenya became a republic. We began the United Advance in Kenya to develop African leadership in many facets of church life and witness. We had to develop new bylaws that would enable the Kenya church to hold property, and to develop the work so that an African could become the chief executive in place of the mission secretary, who had done this for many years. The Advance program was divided into many segments of special training that would prepare the church to take over. A different financial system was developed, both in helping the African church to raise more money itself for its work.

A plan was established by which the Missionary Board would gradually work itself out of being the chief benefactor. The Kenya church and Missionary Board would form a partnership that would cover at least fifteen years. In the beginning, the Missionary Board would supply the much larger share of the finances to operate the work of the mission and church. Year by year, the Missionary Board's share would decrease a little and the Kenya church's part would increase. An African was appointed to become treasurer and an African was chosen by the church to become its executive secretary. Gradually, leadership and responsibility in the Kenya church changed hands. As many more African leaders were trained to carry more responsible jobs, some missionaries were withdrawn and appointed to other fields. By 1967, four years after independence, the Church of God in Kenya had become a registered legal entity and the Missionary Board had agreed to turn over all nonmovable property to the African church in Kenya, including properties related to churches, schools, hospitals, and missionary residences. (One exception is that the missionary residence in Nairobi was still owned by the Missionary Board for several years before being transferred.)

The event of turning over the main responsibility of the Missionary Board work and the deeds to the properties was a big affair in the life of the Kenya church and in the community as a whole. A special day in February 1972 was set by the mission and the church leaders to officially transfer the properties at the large church building at Kima. Many government leaders were invited to the service as well as church leaders from other denominations in the area. It was a great day for the church and the mission. We do not talk anymore about the Mission of the Church of God in Kenya. Rather we talk now *about the Church of God in Kenya in the same way as we talk about the Church of God in the United States, Germany, or elsewhere.*

*Since 1972 when the mission in Kenya became the Kenya church, many situations have developed. The Missionary Board has been responsive to requests to develop an ongoing financial program and establish a solid pension plan for pastors, hospital administration, and the like. The church is gaining strength in its evangelistic outreach and growth. In 1962 the membership of the church was about thirty thousand Christians. Today it is about seventy-five thousand. In those days we had 240 congregations and now more than 400.*

## Outreach in Uganda

Much of the outreach ministry in East Africa during the later years was done by the African people themselves. African Christians, mainly from rural areas, were ever on the move to urban areas in search of employment, many times to neighboring Uganda where they sometimes would find work. As they moved, they carried along with them their Church of God heritage. Their special tribal heritage got them together and in this way other Church of God congregations sprang up. Some of these were in Uganda. During the devastating days of Idi Amin, the dictator, with his cruel and tyrannical ways, our church people had to flee for their lives back to Kenya, and this brought a temporary end to our work in Uganda.

## Outreach in Tanzania

In 1958 two missionary families from Canada, working with an independent missionary program, took up work in remote places near the Great North Road that goes to South Africa. They soon learned the native language and built mission stations in several places. However, after being there a while, they learned about the Church of God missionaries in Kenya who were working with the Missionary Board. In the mid sixties, the Christians of Tanzania officially took their stand with the Church of God in Kenya and all worked in cooperation with the Missionary Board in the United States. While the Christians in the two countries work together in a general way, each had its own organization for operation and outreach. Missionaries have still been needed to help with church development and outreach in Tanzania, but, as a whole, the Church of God work in Tanzania has been gaining strength and reaching new areas.

## United Advance

The United Advance covered five years and a part of the program is still being used. One of the biggest problems we had in helping the church to become self-reliant was to help the people believe in themselves. They had to learn that God was as near to them in Africa to help them as he was to their brothers and sisters across the ocean. Again, I think nationalism had a lot to do with helping the church people to see what was going on in the United States and this motivated many of them to see the necessity for change.

In 1962, Clair and Retha Shultz went to Kenya to assume the responsibilities of mission secretary. This was at a transition period in policies from the British Kenya Colony to the present independent Kenya government. Clair and Retha led the African church through this very difficult period by reorganizing the bylaws for the African Assembly and, later, by turning the mission over to the East African Church of God. They returned to America in 1970.

## Chapter 53

# The New East African Church of God

I was privileged to know many of the first Christians during my years in Africa. I remember Atetwi (Mariamu Jerimiah), the first girl to be baptized. Stephano, Matthayo, Peter, Hannah, Philip, and many others walked and talked with the first missionaries.

Most of them have now died. They lived and contributed to the growth of the church as they influenced others to follow. Mariamu became one of the first teachers, teaching the first consonant and vowel sounds preliminary to reading. Enoch Olando and Zakayo Mulembe were two of the first missionaries who went forth into the Kisa and Ingotse areas.

The state we have now reached has not been acquired in a day. It has been the product of years and years of progress, moving slowly but constantly gaining ground. Oftentimes it was so slow that there was no clear evidence of growth, but it was there just the same.

Since the beginning of the mission, I found that all the missionaries combined exceeded a thousand years of service for the advancement of God's kingdom. As they worked, they shared their skills with their students. The Missionary Board was ever conscious of the growing needs of the African church and, as missionaries were replaced from one field, other greater skills were added to accommodate the growing needs of the people.

We were privileged to see the African people develop one of the strongest powers ever known. Why? Because the love of God changed them.

A few years ago when we went to Kisii, we could not find enough elementary teachers to fill the vacancies in the three schools. Bunyore supplied them. Today a Kisii man, Nelson Obowge, is principal of our Kima Theological College. They moved forward by applying themselves and dedicating themselves to the work to which God called them.

I wrote to Benson Ndebe, one of my former students in Kima Theological College, and asked him to share with us some of the progress the Kenya church has made since becoming an African church. Truly they have become a missionary-minded church and may eventually develop a missionary board for outreach alone.

Benson writes of this church, quoting from a booklet prepared by Byrum Makokha for the African church's Diamond Jubilee:

*Our major goal for the church is to teach the gospel of Christ to the unreached and to equip more leaders for the effective ministry of the church. Our vision goes beyond the East African countries to Central and West Africa where we have good signs of the work to be established. Because our financial resources are limited, we are beginning to make plans to establish some income-generating projects that could become sources of income for the support of the church's ministry.*

### Churches

*Presently we have more than four hundred fifty churches. The majority of these churches are within the western part of Kenya. The number of our city churches has grown to thirty-eight, including those of Nairobi. Out of these city churches, only eight have church buildings. Due to the expansion of our churches in the cities, we have a missionary couple, Robert and Janet Edwards, who are directors of the urban development program.*

### Kisii

*Our ministry in Kisii has expanded to thirty-two churches. Some of them have no trained ministers, but with the reopening* of Ibeno Bible School, we trust that many will be equipped for effective ministry in the Kisii area. (The Masai hope to attend the Bible school at Ibeno, Kisii.)

## Masai

God had indeed blessed our outreach ministry in Masailand where we have twenty churches, most of them pastored by the Masai pastors. We have established ten primary schools and six clinics in the Masai area. We have such a wide-open door for spreading the gospel in Masai and we praise God for that.

## Bukhayo

Our outreach ministry is Bukhayo and Teso is expanding. Presently we have fifteen churches in the Bukhayo and Teso area.

## Education

We have more than one hundred primary schools and thirty secondary schools, five of which are government maintained. The two who have forms V and VI (junior college level) are Bunyore Girls High School and Emusire High School.

## Local Village Churches

God is blessing in our local village churches. They are growing spiritually and in giving for the Lord's work.

## Kima Theological College

The ministry at Kima Theological College is expanding. We have fifty resident students including six women who have dedicated themselves to prepare for the church's ministry. Three of the resident students are from Zaire. In addition to the students, twenty-six candidates for ordination are being trained at Kima Theological College for two terms before their ordination this year in August.

## Extension Program

The Theological Education by Extension program (TEE) has grown so much that we have five-hundred students under this program. These classes are carried on in the villages under the leadership of the college faculty or graduates. Classes are held each week. We have the following full-time personnel at Kima Theological College:

| | |
|---|---|
| Nelson Obwoge | Principal |
| Naftali Tsumah | Academic Dean |
| Nassar Farag | Tutor |

| *Nova Hutchins* | *Tutor* |
| *Frances Kiboi* | *Tutor* |

## Clinics and Hospitals

In addition, an extensive medical program comprising clinics and two hospitals has been a significant part of the African church's ministry.

We are proud of this fine leadership in the African church. These men have ventured out into the United States or Europe and received their education. I am sure that many times in acquiring their education away from home, they have sacrificed their families and have been desperately lonely, but they persevered and now so many young people will gain by their sacrifice.

## To the East Africa Church of God

May God bless you as you pursue your major goal. There is no limit in God's work. Our prayers are behind you. We as missionaries have done what we could and have laid down our working tools, but you have yet so many years ahead of you. Use them for God's work and you will never have any regrets. As we look back over our lives spent with you, we see you have made them joyous years because you have not turned away but have advanced to the place where you can do so much more than we would have been able to do. Now our ministry for you will be that of prayer.

May God bless you.

# Chronology

1904  Robert Wilson explores the new site for a mission

05  The Robert Wilsons return to begin the South African Compounds and Interior Mission at Bunyore

Mr. Bernston arrives to help with building

07  Johanna Bila, a South African, arrives from the Zulu tribe in South Africa

Emusire Mission opens with Swedish missionaries at Ebudongoi

Mr. Richardson comes from Australia to join the mission

10  Johanna Bila dies and is buried at Kima

Joseph Nyambele, a South African, comes to replace Bila

10  Robert Wilson retires because of ill health

11  Richardson baptizes the first two converts

12  Richardson baptizes 13 candidates, one of whom was the first girl to be baptized

14  Mabel Baker comes to the mission with her father A. W. Baker and remains as a missionary for 39 years

Richardson dies in the Congo

Henry Kramer assumes Mr. Richardson's work

15  Mr. Dalziel comes for a short time, but leaves when the war begins, being a conscientious objector

21  O. C. Keller serves when Henry and Gertrude Kramer go on furlough

Ingotse mission begins

James Murray arrives in Kenya

22  Ruth Fisher comes to Kima

Henry and Gertrude Kramer return

The Samuel Joiners come to Kima

22  South Africa Compound Mission is Given to Church of God

23  Boys School begins at Kima

24  William and Lilly Bailey go to Ingotse

25  James Murray and Ruth Fisher are married

27  John and Twyla Ludwig arrive in Kenya
    Henry and Gertrude Kramer retire from mission
    Printing press installed at Kima
28  Twyla Ludwig opens dispensary and hospital at Kima
34  Sidney and Fern Rogers become principal of the Kima Boys
    Kisa Mission is started by the U.S. Women of the Church of God.
    James and Ruth Murray go to Ingotse
35  Freda Strenger comes to Kima Hospital
36  Ruth Fisher Murray dies of typhoid fever
    Lima Lehmer comes to school and hospital at Kima
37  Homer and Vivian Bailey go to Kisa
38  John and Twyla Ludwig go on first furlough after serving for 12 years in Kenya Colony
39  World War II begins
40  Ludwigs return from furlough in August
    James T. Murray dies
44  Sidney and Fern Rogers leave for furlough after 10 years
    Jewell Hall comes to relieve Lima Lehmer
45  E. A. and Pearl Reardon arrive in Kenya
    Herman and Lavera Smith arrive as secretary of the mission
46  Ruth Sanderson and Lima Lehmer come to Kenya
    Mabel Baker leaves on furlough
    Frank and Margret LaFont arrive at Kima
47  Ruben and Nora Schwieger arrive as principal of boys school.
    Irene Engst comes to Mwihila as a nurse
    Teacher training center begins at Mwihila
49  Lydia Hansen replaces Ruth Sanderson at Kima
50  David and Elsie Gaulke arrive from China.
    Schwiegers move to Ingotse
    Women's weekly Bible classes begin in the Bunyore churches
    Ludwigs retire in Nairobi and open an independent mission
    First trip to Kisii is made by the Bunyore church
    Calvin and Martha Braillier arrive as secretary of education
    Kima Hospital is dedicated
51  Wick and Grace Donohew arrive at Kima
52  Jane Ryan goes to Ingotse as a nurse

234

Velma Schneider comes to the Bunyore girls school at Kima

James and Glenna Yutzy come to the teacher training center at Kisa (Mwihila) as principal.

53 David and Elsie Gaulke return to Mwihila to begin the hospital work

Frank LaFont builds the teacher training center at Mwihila

Mabel Baker retires after 39 years

Carl and Eva-Clare Kardatzke arrive on Fulbright Scholarship

Dr. and Mrs. A. F. Gray arrive in Kenya

Wick Donohew begins Kima Bible School

54 Dedication of the Luyia New Testament with the Psalms

Vera Martin arrives at Mwihila Hospital

55 GOLDEN JUBILEE with special guests Adam Miller, Lester Crose, and Mabel Baker

Naomi Sweeny arrives at Mwihila Hospital

Frank LaFont supervises building of hospital complex

Merlene Huber arrives as lab technician for Mwihila

56 DEDICATION OF THE MWIHILA HOSPITAL

David and Joan Livingston come to Mwihila Hospital

Richard and Donna Smith arrive at Mwihila Hospital

Rosa Bollmeyer comes to Kima as nurse

Lew and Wanda Goodrich arrive at the Bible School

Dedication of the Kaloleni church in Nairobi

C. Jean Kilmer and Ruth come from Egypt for a short term

58 Vivian Phelps comes as teacher at Baker Elementary School

Dedication of the Baker Elementary School for children of missionaries

David and Elsie Gaulke retire from Mwihila Hospital

Donohews go on furlough

Sam and Jane Betts come to Kisii

Ibeno Mission opens

Harley and Bonnie Richardson arrive as maintenance personnel

59 Delores Beatty comes to Mwihila Hospital

60 Doug and Ruth Welch come to Mwihila

Edna Thimes comes to Kima as a nurse

Harold and Donna LaFont go to Mwihila Hospital

Darlene Detweiler goes to Mwihila Hospital

61 Lima Lehmer retires

Arthenia Turner comes to Mwihila Hospital
Simon and Mae Robinson come to Kisii
James and Dorothy Sharp go to Mwihila High School
as principal
High school started at Mwihila; teacher training phased
out
First African, Daudi Otieno, appointed chairperson of
African General Assembly
62 Esther Beaty goes to Kima Girls School
Richard and Georgia Woodsome go to Emusire High
School
Candance Heinley goes to Mwihila and Ibeno as a
nurse
Wick and Grace Donohew retire
63 KENYA GAINS HER INDEPENDENCE
Ruben Don and Virginia Schwieger go to Mwihila High
School
High School begins at Emusire
64 Harry and Jene Nachtigall go to Emusire
Oscar and Norma Borden assigned to Kima
James and Elizabeth Royster go to Kima for one year
65 Dennis and Elaine Habel assigned to Mwihila
66 Lew and Wanda Goodrick leave Kenya
Edgar and Lima Williams assigned to Kima Theological
College
67 Cornelia Barnett assigned to hospital
David and Karen Crippen assigned to curriculum
development
William and Beatrice Anderson assigned to Mwihila
Hospital
68 Janice Linamen goes to Mwihila Hospital
Jan Dazley serves as teacher for missionary children
Roger and Margaret Bruce assigned to Mwihila Hospital
69 Howard and Mary Hutton arrive at Mwihila

70 Caroline Ackerman serves at Mwihila Hospital
Margaret Deitz serves at Mwihila Hospital
Aaron and Kathryn Kerr become hospital administrator
Margaret and David Montague serve at Kima Theo-
logical College
Vivian Woods goes to Mwihila Hospital
Edgar and Lima Williams retire
Byron Makokha becomes first African treasurer of
General Assembly
Clair and Retha Shultz leave Kenya

## Short Term Teachers

| | |
|---|---|
| Burns, Glenn and Francine | 73-77 |
| Cummins, Kay | 69-75 |
| Dunham, Barbara | 67-70 |
| Edwards, Robert and Janet | 67-69 |
| Fuller, Douglas and Dontie | 72-74 |
| Gard, Diana | 69 |
| Harting, Clyde and Rowena | 65-69 |
| Humes, Mary Lou | 67-69 |
| King, Linda | 68-70 |
| Newberry, Gene and Agnes | 73-74 |
| Railey, Robert | 66-69 |
| Roberts, Pamela | 69-71 |
| Saltzmann, Paul | 66-68 |
| Tefft, Ruthann | 69-71 and 74-75 |
| Upchurch, Caroline | 64-69 |
| Von Bargen, Daniel | 67-69 |
| Ward, Sheryl | 67-69 |

# Epilogue

Benson Ndebe gave us a partial picture of the church today with its phenomenal growth as it reaches out beyond its borders. One of the most rewarding aspects of my returning to Kenya in 1966 was to find six of the fine, young Kisii men in Kima Theological College studying for the ministry. Nelson Obwoge is now serving as the principal of the college and Jackson Bosire will head up the extension course held at the Ibeno Mission for the Masai ministers. Twenty years ago we had to borrow teachers from Bunyore to operate our Kisii schools; now, Christians from Kisii have obtained higher education overseas with which to serve the church.

I have purposely not touched the program of the contemporary church since I lack firsthand knowledge. I would certainly hope that some who have experienced the recent years of transition that have occurred in Kenya may take the story on from 1970 and compile a sequel to this writing with current experiences and information.